The Phenomenology of Love
and Reading

The Phenomenology of Love and Reading

Cassandra Falke

Bloomsbury Academic
An imprint of Bloomsbury Publishing Inc

B L O O M S B U R Y
NEW YORK · LONDON · OXFORD · NEW DELHI · SYDNEY

Bloomsbury Academic
An imprint of Bloomsbury Publishing Inc

1385 Broadway	50 Bedford Square
New York	London
NY 10018	WC1B 3DP
USA	UK

www.bloomsbury.com

BLOOMSBURY and the Diana logo are trademarks of Bloomsbury Publishing Plc

First published 2017

© Cassandra Falke, 2017

British Library Cataloguing-in-Publication Data
A catalogue record for this book is available from the British Library.

ISBN: HB: 978-1-6289-2648-4
ePub: 978-1-6289-2650-7
ePDF: 978-1-6289-2649-1

Library of Congress Cataloging-in-Publication Data
Names: Falke, Cassandra, author.
Title: The phenomenology of love and reading / Cassandra Falke. Description: New York : Bloomsbury Academic, 2016. | Includes bibliographical references and index.
Identifiers: LCCN 2016017286 (print) | LCCN 2016029391 (ebook) | ISBN 9781628926484 (hardback) | ISBN 9781628926507 (ePub) | ISBN 9781628926491 (ePDF)
Subjects: LCSH: Phenomenology and literature. | Marion, Jean-Luc, 1946—Criticism and interpretation. | Love. | Books and reading. | Literature–Philosophy. | Literature–Psychology. | Literature–History and criticism. | BISAC: LITERARY CRITICISM / Semiotics & Theory. | LITERARY CRITICISM / Books & Reading. | PHILOSOPHY / Ethics & Moral Philosophy.
Classification: LCC PN49 .F35 2016 (print) | LCC PN49 (ebook) | DDC 809/.93353–dc23
LC record available at https://lccn.loc.gov/2016017286

Cover design: Hugh Cowling

Typeset by Newgen Knowledge Works (P) Ltd., Chennai, India
Printed and bound in the United States of America

Contents

Acknowledgments

The nature of this book's subject makes it impossible for me to thank, or even recognize, all who have influenced my thinking about it. Damon, Charlie, and Sebastian have encouraged and inspired me daily throughout the process of writing. My students, in particular those who studied literary theory with me in 2012 and 2015, have helped me refine my ideas and have established the standard of clarity that I aim to meet in my writing. Don Rhea, Judy, Dennis, and the Middletons have offered the space and sense of home that I needed in order to be productive. The efficient and always pleasant staff of Bloomsbury Academic Publishers must include many people who deserve thanks, whose names I do not know, but I am happy to thank, by name, Haaris and Mary for their faith in this project. Bloomsbury's anonymous readers offered extremely helpful feedback and shaped the book's development in crucial ways. I am grateful, too, for their time and attention.

Material support for the project is easier to trace. I would like to thank the US-Norway Fulbright Foundation and East Texas Baptist University for supporting a concentrated period of work on the book in 2013 and 2014. The University of Bergen, East Texas Baptist University, and the University of Tromsø have also provided essential support in the form of conference stipends and congenial working environments.

I am grateful to the literary estates of Dudley Randall and e. e. cummings for permission to reprint their work:

Introduction

In Jean-Luc Marion's thinking, we are a bedazzled people. The unfurling of events, the encounter with art, the experience of flesh itself, and the meeting of another's gaze reveal our good fortune to be the recipients of innumerable gifts—more than we could have imagined, more than we can take in, a number dumfounding the question of use. For the last twenty years,[1] Marion has characterized our days and nights as a series of "saturated phenomena" where the event, artwork, flesh, or face that gives itself to us overwhelms our capacity to experience it and in the process reconstitutes our capacities to expect, receive, and express more givenness. In the last ten years he has named the force through which we are made and remade "love." He calls the view that we become ourselves through our loves and hates "the erotic reduction."[2]

The Phenomenology of Love and Reading examines the implications of the erotic reduction for literary theory. In Marion's phenomenology, love overcomes the vanity of what he calls the "epistemic" and "ontological" reductions. Assuring ourselves of our own being through cognition or awareness of *ipseity* cannot, Marion argues, provide us with any reason to *want* to be. Only loving

---

[1] Marion first wrote about the saturated phenomenon in 1992, in a contribution to a volume entitled *Phénomène et théologie*, to which Jean-Louis Chrétien, Michel Henry, and Paul Ricoeur also contributed. His essay for this volume, called "The Saturated Phenomenon" appeared in English in 2000 as part of *Phenomenology and the "Theological Turn": The French Debate*. He also contributed the article "The Saturated Phenomenon" to *Philosophy Today* (40, no. 1 [1996]: 103–124). In 2001, Marion explored the concept more fully in his book *In Excess: Studies of Saturated Phenomena*, trans. Robyn Horner and Vincent Berraud (New York: Fordham University Press, 2002).

[2] Marion fully articulates the erotic reduction in *The Erotic Phenomenon*, trans. Stephen E. Lewis (Chicago: University of Chicago Press, 2007), originally published as *Le Phénomène Érotique* (2003), and hereafter referred to in the text as *EP*. He had also discussed love earlier in *Prolegomena to Charity*, trans. Stephen E. Lewis (New York: Fordham University Press, 2002), originally published as *Prolégomènes à la Charité* (1986).

and the hope of being loved adds purpose to the impoverished certainty that we can arrive at alone (*EP* 21–23). Reading that is trapped in epistemology and ontology is similarly impoverished. Reading within the epistemic reduction, we may acquire knowledge, even knowledge about how to love others, but the epistemic reduction provides no bridge between knowing how to love and actually loving. The ontological reduction can account for the ways that reading changes us individually but not for the relationship between us as readers and other people.

The propulsion from the world of a book into the world of others, which is so essential for the erotic phenomenon, helps overcome the gap between the cry in literature and "the cry in the street" that has undermined some critics' hope for an ethics of reading. George Steiner asks in *Real Presences*, "Does the cry in the tragic play muffle, even blot out, the cry in the street?" He confesses to finding this an "obsessive, almost maddening question" and cites Samuel Taylor Coleridge, who wrote in his notebook that "poetry excites us to artificial feelings—makes us callous to real ones."[3] Similarly, Suzanne Keen worries in her 2007 book *Empathy and the Novel* that "the very fictionality of novels predisposes readers to empathize with characters, since a fiction known to be 'made up' does not activate suspicion and wariness as an apparently 'real' appeal for assistance may do."[4] Steiner, Coleridge, and Keen are right to express this concern. The act of reading does not guarantee a future ethical action. No act in the present does. Within the erotic reduction, loving acts expand us—like rain expands a river or variation expands music—and all that follows is shaped by their entrance into our lives, if not always in predictable ways. Therefore, to whatever extent reading includes actions that are part of love, to that extent it changes us. These actions, like love itself, involve, not the assertion of will or harvesting of knowledge that one might expect in reading oriented toward ontology or epistemology, but rather attention, empathy, and a willingness to be overwhelmed.

If "the point is to love, because under the rules of the erotic reduction, nothing unloved or unloving holds" (*EP* 28), then why read at all? Should we

---

[3] George Steiner, *Real Presences* (Chicago: University of Chicago Press, 1991), 144.
[4] Suzanne Keen, *Empathy and the Novel* (Oxford: Oxford University Press, 2007), 4.

not be busy feeding the hungry or kissing on the couch? Within the erotic reduction, those are indeed worthy activities that "hold," but I will argue that reading is one as well. In entering the erotic reduction, the crucial requirement is that I am "susceptible to a decision, which does not belong to me and which determines me in advance, because it comes to me from elsewhere" (*EP* 25). Books provide an elsewhere. Reading literature, I argue, unfolds with the singularity of an act of love, and like an act of love requires us to yield our intention.[5]

The event of reading, like the event of loving, is singular. Just as our love for another creates a new reality as it unfolds, each reading of a particular text makes us lovers without precedent. Reading creates in us new ways of loving, and thus new ways of being. Or it can. In order for a book to work on us this way, we have to open ourselves up to an intentionality and signifying practice that originates outside of our own "egological sphere" (*EP* 102). Because we cannot anticipate the way we will be changed by an event of reading, we commit ourselves first to the act of surrender itself and, through that surrender of our own intentionality, find ourselves remade.

The first section of the book considers themes from previous phenomenological thinking about reading that might become part of what Rita Felski calls a "new phenomenological turn" in literary criticism.[6] This clarifies the contribution that Marion's philosophy makes to a practice almost a century old while also reviving some phenomenological practices of reading that have been neglected. I then provide an overview of the "erotic reduction," suggesting parallels between the ways we engage another person through love and the ways we engage with a book. I will end the book's first section by describing what Marion calls "the lover's advance," the moment when we forget ourselves and love first. Modern reading is a solitary activity, and without the presence of another person who could potentially love us back, we cannot complete the erotic phenomenon. But, the alterity we find in books imitates the alterity of the beloved enough to train us in the act of loving first.

[5] I use the word "singularity" with reference to Derek Attridge's *The Singularity of Literature* (London: Routledge, 2004) and also to Marion's description of "singular" events, e.g., in *Being Given: Toward a Phenomenology of Givenness*, trans. Jeffrey L. Kosky (Stanford: Stanford University Press, 2002), 139.

[6] Rita Felski, *The Uses of Literature* (Oxford: Blackwell, 2008), 18.

The second section of the book takes up the habits of love in which reading trains us. I suggest that reading literature can develop the habits of attention and empathy. By "habit" I do not mean something we do unawares, such as the habit of sleeping on my right side. I mean "habit" in the sense that a habit of walking a particular path in the woods creates that path and enables one to walk it more easily next time. In addition to the habits of attention and empathy, reading can also develop readers' willingness to cede control and experience the saturated phenomenon of "the sublime, pleasure, the beautiful or love."[7] Everyone, according to Marion, experiences the dazzle of saturated phenomena. Everyone can be caught off guard by love or beauty, but in his discussions of painting, Marion models a kind of intentionality that allows for our experiences of saturated phenomenon to be more constitutive. By examining Marion's own practice here and describing what a comparable practice would look like for literature, I foreground pre- and post-reading reflection. This balances the discussion of attentive and empathetic practices that readers perform while still immersed in books and opens up an area of inquiry for ethical criticism that has been curiously taken for granted.

I should anticipate up front two objections to my argument that reading can make us better lovers. First, there are the twin perils of normativity and moral relativism. The worry over these problems assumes an epistemological virtue ethics that the erotic construction of the self avoids. Marion explains that worrying over the sturdiness or flimsiness of a moral law does not make sense within the erotic reduction because "such a law [would] mask the other by lowering him or her to the rank of a simple opportunity among others to obey the law" (*EP* 213). An approach to reading based on the erotic reduction does not aim to make a reader more adept at applying a moral law, but aims to make him or her more open to the new possibilities of love that another individual will offer. It thereby avoids the charge of ethical normativity sometimes levied against criticism that sees literature as valuable for human relationships. The ghostly opposite of normativity, relativism, also fails to describe the growth in love that this reading approach aspires to because it also presumes a law-based

---

[7] Jean-Luc Marion, *The Crossing of the Visible*, trans. James K. A. Smith (Stanford: Stanford University Press, 2004), 56.

ethic, a thing transcending relationships that can be altered relative to a given situation. The reader in pursuit of love "acquires an ethical privilege," not by meeting a preconceived ethical requirement or foisting an ethical evaluation upon a given situation, but by allowing himself or herself to be "altered from elsewhere and opened by it" (*EP* 25). Each moment of such alteration, be it from a book or a beloved, transpires as a singular and creative event. By describing our interdependence on others, the erotic reduction cannot, of course, make anyone more loving who does not want to become more loving. But, if we accept that the basis of all our lives *is* love and begin *within* the erotic reduction seeking ways to have more of the life that love offers us, then literature operates with an ethical force upon the selves that we are continually becoming.

Another objection—that we cannot really love through books the way we love through people—I fully accept. In concluding Chapter 6, I discuss the flesh and why the completion of the erotic reduction presumes the presence of an embodied beloved. The significance of this point should not be overlooked because it is the bridge that allows our actions as readers to be meaningful in the rest of our lives. We can only really love other people. As obvious as this statement may sound, it is worth making. Phenomenological explorations of literature have thus far skirted the question of what difference our bodies make to us as readers by referring to persons only as so many disembodied consciousnesses. This implicit disembodiment of people makes the case for a book's shaping us as though it were a person *during a reading* more compelling, but then we must stop reading to eat lunch, maybe with a real friend. The erotic reduction can be fulfilled at lunch with a friend, at home with a lover, by the fjord with my (specific) boy in my (specific) lap. It can be fulfilled in an inspiring diversity of ways, but it cannot be fulfilled by means of reading. The crossings of the lovers' gaze and and the lovers' flesh operate as powerful figures in *The Erotic Phenomenon*. As figures, their incarnated performance reminds us of the interdependence and radical passivity of love. But they are more than figures. As events, the crossing of the gaze and the crossing of the flesh are essential to the completion of the erotic phenomenon. Marion writes that "without this shared eroticization" love's oath would remain "an abstract linguistic performance, which would not phenomenalize itself anywhere and would not individualize me any more than anyone else" (*EP* 121). The language and physical body of a book can never offer the uniqueness of the flesh through which the erotic reduction may be fully accomplished. Lacking the ability to deny our advance, lacking flesh, lacking the uniqueness of an embodied person, a book cannot help us complete the erotic reduction that it helped us begin.

Introducing Marion

Jean-Luc Marion needs no introduction in the world of philosophy.[8] Since 2004 he has been a Professor of Catholic Studies and Professor of the Philosophy of Religions and Theology at the University of Chicago. He preceded that with eight years as the Director of Philosophy at the Sorbonne. He was elected an *immortel* by the Académie française in 2008. He is the author of twenty-seven books covering Cartesian thought, the history of philosophy, theology, and phenomenology as well as articles, edited collections, and conference papers on these topics running into the hundreds. Brian Robinette calls him "one of the most important and theologically fertile thinkers within the phenomenological tradition," and Ian James credits him with "redefine[ing] the terms of philosophical debate in France in the wake of deconstruction and the 'death of the subject.'"[9]

In spite of his recognition as a philosopher, the value of his work to literature has not yet been recognized among English readers. Whereas his phenomenological predecessors Jacques Derrida, Emmanuel Lévinas, and Paul Ricoeur have received the attention of literary scholars, Marion has not. In part, this lack is attributable to Marion's youth. A student of Derrida and an academic successor to both Lévinas and Ricoeur, Marion represents a new generation of phenomenology.[10] It naturally takes time for discourses that

---

[8] For more a more detailed introduction to Marion's work, see Kevin Hart, "Introduction," *Jean-Luc Marion: The Essential Writings*, ed. Kevin Hart (New York: Fordham University Press, 2013).

[9] Brian Robinette, "A Gift to Theology? Jean-Luc Marion's 'Saturated Phenomenon' in Christological Perspective," *Heythrop Journal* 48, no. 1 (2007): 86; and, Ian James, *The New French Philosophy* (London: Polity Press, 2012), 18.

[10] For a biographical overview of Marion's relationships with these three predecessors, see Robyn Horner, *Jean-Luc Marion: A Theological Introduction* (Aldershot: Ashgate Press, 2005), 3–12. For

begin in one discipline to move to another, and Marion's most relevant works for literary studies—*In Excess: Studies of Saturated Phenomena, The Crossing of the Visible*, and *The Erotic Phenomenon*—have all been written within the last fifteen years. It also takes time for work to move from one language to another. Of the sixteen books by Marion now available in English, twelve of them have been released since the year 2000.[11] Although several translators are now committed to making Marion's work available in English, the processes of translation and republication necessarily takes time. Additionally, whereas Ricoeur and Derrida wrote explicitly about reading, Marion had not done so before his publication of *In the Self's Place: The Approach of Saint Augustine*, which appeared in French in 2008 and in English in 2012. And, although he has taught phenomenology and painting at the University of Chicago, there has been no institutional link between his phenomenological writings and the practice of literary criticism as there was for Derrida and Ricoeur. Nevertheless, it is uncharacteristic that literary critics have not worked more at the theoretical level with the new generation of phenomenologists. As Kevin Hart notes, "Literary criticism, which has never been shy of gleaning from adjacent disciplines, has not yet taken what it needs from the current generation of French phenomenologists, even when we are told that phenomenology is without limits and therefore perfectly able to be at home in talk about writing and reading literature."[12]

Another possible reason for the silence about Marion in literary criticism is his association with a "theological turn" supposedly leading phenomenology away from its origin. In 1991, the French Heidegger specialist Dominique Janicaud accused Marion, Lévinas, Michel Henry, and Jean-Louis Chrétien of committing "treason [against] the reduction" that initiated phenomenology by opening phenomenology up to the possibility of a force or being beyond our perception.[13] Janicaud says that this force or being is assumed to be the

---

an account of his intellectual relationship with them, see James, *The New French Philosophy* and Hart, "Introduction," *Essential Writings*.

[11] For a bibliography of Marion's work, see Hart, *Essential Writings*.

[12] Kevin Hart, "Afterword," *Christianity and Literature* 58, no. 2 (2009): 298.

[13] Dominique Janicaud et al., *Phenomenology and the Theological Turn: The French Debate* (Fordham: Fordham University Press, 2000), 27. The volume contains Janicauld's "The Theological Turn in French Phenomenology," originally issued in French as a report to the International Institute of Philosophy in 1991 (trans. Bernard G. Prusak), which makes the accusation, and responses from Marion, Ricoeur, Henry, Chrétien, and Jean-François Courtine.

biblical God with no phenomenological verification. This accusation need not condemn these thinkers to isolation from literary theory. Indeed, over the last decade, literary theory has opened itself up to the "post-secular turn" heralded by Habermas and attended to by scholars of theology, feminism, and political theory.[14] The phenomenologists Janicaud denounces as theologically motivated were in fact receiving attention from literary theorists even before that. Just at the time that Janicaud issued his complaint in France, Jill Robbins and Robert Eaglestone in America and England were fruitfully exploring the relevance of Lévinasian ethics to reading literature, and Ricoeur was patiently producing work that illuminated a hermeneutic circle between literature and life.[15]

There are signs that literary scholars have renewed their attention to the connection between literature and the rest of life that the concepts of saturated phenomenality and the erotic reduction can provide. The assumption that literature was part of an influential cultural matrix in the past is commonplace, but scholars are increasingly open to reexamining reading's relevance for life in the present. Marion's generation of French thinkers depart from the "linguistic, textual or discursive paradigm of (post-) structuralism," and seek instead to engage with those elements of life that exceed language's limits and persist in spite of their unsayability.[16] Like the new French philosophers, literary theorists are shaking off linguistic confines. One might even say that there is a sense of relief and playfulness in critics looking for the actions and possibilities language cannot contain, as when Joshua Landy writes that "all of us could do with returning to the wisdom of Wordsworth, Schopenhauer

---

[14] Jürgen Habermas, "Secularism's Crisis of Faith: Notes on Post-Secular Society," *New Perspectives Quarterly* 25 (2008): 17–29. For an overview of the trend away from secularity, see Gregor McLennen, "The Postsecular Turn," *Theory, Culture & Society* 27, no. 4 (July 2010): 3–20.

[15] On Lévinasian ethics and literature, see Jill Robbins, *Altered Reading: Levinas and Literature* (Chicago: University of Chicago, 1999); Robert Eaglestone, *Ethical Criticism: Reading after Levinas* (Edinburgh: Edinburgh University Press, 1997). See also, Donald R. Wehrs, *Levinas and Twentieth-Century Literature: Ethics and the Reconstitution of Subjectivity* (Newark: University of Delaware Press, 2013); and Colin Davis, *Critical Excess: Overreading in Derrida, Deleuze, Levinas, Žižek and Cavell* (Stanford: Stanford University Press, 2010). Ricoeur's work in the years surrounding Janicaud's accusation includes *From Text to Action: Essays in Hermeneutics II*, trans. Kathleen Blamey and John B. Thompson (Evanston: Northwestern University Press, 1991); *Oneself as Another*, trans. Kathleen Blamey (Chicago: University of Chicago Press, 1992); and *Critique and Conviction*, trans. Kathleen Blamey (New York: Columbia University Press, 1998). For a summary of Ricoeur's influence in literary criticism, see Sophie Vlacos, *Ricoeur, Literature and Imagination* (New York: Bloomsbury Press, 2014).

[16] James, *The New French Philosophy*, 5–12.

and company, lovers of art, who eschewed semantics in favor of pragmatics. We could do, in other words, with ceasing to talk about what a text 'says'— if indeed there is such a thing—and beginning to talk about what it *does*."[17] Marion's work provides a wonderful connection between new discourses in phenomenology and new discourses in literature because it clarifies the basis from which all our doing arises, which is love.

An approach to literature informed by Marion's phenomenology must begin with a focus on givenness. The givenness of what we are and what we experience provides the grounding of Marion's philosophy, and he points out that phenomenology has always had gift as its foundation. For him, givenness precedes both knowledge and being, and the phenomenological reduction (wherein we step outside of the "natural" belief that we can separate the perceiving self from what it perceives) begins with the recognition of givenness: "No givenness without reduction, no reduction that does not lead to a givenness."[18] In terms of literary criticism, accepting the givenness of a text implies two things—first, a charitable acceptance of a text as gift and, second, a recognition of the otherness of the text as both unavoidable and productive. Charitable reading has roots in both philosophy and theology. Within philosophy, the principle of charity suggests that a reader construes an author's argument in the most reasonable and positive terms and then engages with that strong version.[19] Theologically, charity underpins all virtuous activity as the spirit of God acting through believers. Charitable reading thus implies a generous construal of a text's meaning and form performed in the confidence that such an interpretation flows from and contributes to the love we enact in the rest of our lives.[20]

Thinking about a text's givenness also calls to mind its essential otherness. Every gift originates from elsewhere. For a work of literature, this "elsewhere"

---

[17] Joshua Landy, *How to Do Things with Fictions* (Oxford: Oxford University Press, 2012), 9.
[18] Marion, *In Excess*, 18.
[19] For philosophically oriented charitable reading, see Donald Davidson, *Inquiries into Truth and Interpretation* (Oxford: Oxford University Press, 2001).
[20] For more on theologically oriented charitable reading, see Alan Jacobs, *A Theology of Reading: The Hermeneutics of Love* (Boulder: Westview Press, 2001). See also Cassandra Falke, "Good Reading: An Ethics of Christian Literary Theory," and Jessica Hooton, "After Theory, After Modernity: Reading Humbly," both in Cassandra Falke, ed. *Intersections in Christianity and Critical Theory* (Basingstoke: Palgrave, 2010).

may become limited in the process of critical inquiry to a focus on the elsewhere of the time and place of composition or the elsewhere of the author's developing oeuvre, but a more profound recognition of otherness acknowledges that we cannot get to the elsewhere from which a text originates. Rather, the alterity of a text provides the opportunity for an event of reading that it singularly makes possible. The distance between what a text offers us and what we bring to a reading is not a gulf to be covered, but a space that shapes an action.

As *adonné*, the gifted, our role as readers and viewers of art is to welcome and acknowledge. As any good host knows, welcoming is not a passive activity. It involves anticipating the guest's/text's arrival in a way that will facilitate the best possible visit. Never ceasing to adjust their preparations as a visit unfolds, good hosts and good readers find their preconceptions of the visit changing while engaging the other as guest. The hermeneutic circle rolls forward in the process of reading as a reader's expectations shape the act of reading and are themselves reshaped. Significantly, the welcoming critic yields mastery over the text. According to Marion, the only mastery that either painter or viewer exercises over the painting "consists, precisely, in letting the unseen burst into the visible by surprise".[21] As readers, too, our responsibility is to be ready for that surprise gift.

The problem of rhetoric

A literary theoretical text about love inevitably runs into problems of rhetoric. Literary inquiry has yet to find the language with which to speak about love. How to avoid the accusation of sentimentality? How to suggest the givenness of phenomenality and the givenness of textual experience without limiting the possibilities of the source of that donation? How to argue for critical reading practices that begin in a totalizing reduction, a mental move that takes in the entirety of perceptual life in one gesture, when most critical reading practices eschew any relationship between reading and the actions and cares that constitute the rest of a reader's life? Even those practices that imply that

[21] Jean-Luc Marion, *The Crossing of the Visible*, trans. James K. A. Smith (Stanford: Stanford University Press, 2004), 32.

reading literature matters for the way readers behave locate the source of transformative power between the covers of a book, where a reader, imagined as a liberal, autonomous subjectivity, can recognize and wield it or ignorantly let it lie. I am thinking of critical approaches that credit literary works with challenging oppressive ideologies. How to write about the experience of reading, and particularly the experience of reading within the erotic reduction, in a way that does not represent the quirks and foibles of a single life of love and reading as normative?

I will try to address these concerns point by point. As Wendy Brown writes in her exploration of the word "critique," criticism seems "to carry the tacit presumption of reason's capacity to unveil error."[22] *The Phenomenology of Love and Reading* proclaims the insufficiency of reason and challenges the presumption that unveiling error is the highest goal of writing about literature. To say that I am critiquing this goal would be to lapse into the logic of critique itself. To effectively challenge critique as Brown defines it, the epistemological focus of "unveiling error" must be replaced by a focus on the practices that a reader and a text can perform together. Seeking error is surely not the most interesting or beneficial of these acts. Stanley Cavell has drawn attention to narration as a critical act, placing his engagements with texts in story forms that facilitate the contemplation of their own intellectual processes and resisting the easy satisfaction of an error exposed. The text that Brown introduces, entitled "Is Critique Secular?" foregrounds inquiry. Rita Felski gives priority to recognition in her *Uses of Literature*. None of these critics abandon reason or reject the possibility that the discourses they respond to might contain errors, but they recall the rich diversity of ways that literary critics could, if we wanted to, invite our readers to think about texts, ways that extend beyond problematizing or exposure. These other critical practices need not be branded as sentimental just because they evoke intellectual processes that are not aggressively argumentative. To oppose reasoned argument only with sentimentality or un-reason would be to turn a blind eye to the manner in which human beings converse with each other all the time. It would be to

[22] Wendy Brown, "Introduction," *Is Critique Secular? Blasphemy, Injury, and Free Speech*, ed. Talal Asad, Wendy Brown, Judith Butler, and Saba Mahmood (Berkeley: Townsend Center for the Humanities, 2009), 9.

lapse into a conceptual dichotomization that is not only pre-Derridian, but unglamorously illogical.

The second concern, about what might exceed textuality and provide a source of givenness, is more complex. There are fewer high-profile critics to point to who embrace the possibility that there *is* something outside the tissues of textuality. Recently, attention has been paid to secularism's confinement of discourse in theory, but the challenges to secularity issued by scholars as diverse as Charles Taylor, Slavoj Žižek, and Roberto Unger, however formidable, have not shaken the confident secularity of much literary critical discourse.[23] Still, literary criticism is ready for Marion. Post-secular stirrings indicate that some scholars feel confined by empiricism on the one hand and a strict textual focus on the other. In 2007, Talal Asad, Saba Mahmood, and Judith Butler joined Brown in asking "Is Critique Secular?" Their examination of dominant secularity at Berkeley's Townsend Center for the Humanities became a book of the same title. The same year, Charles Taylor historicized *The Secular Age*, opening secularity itself up to critique.[24] Luke Ferretter wrote *Towards a Christian Literary Theory* in 2003, and in 2010, *Intersections in Christianity and Critical Theory* brought together twelve scholars exploring the historical interrelationship of Christianity and critical theory as well as the ways that they are enlivening each other in current critical practices.[25] God was denounced by Marx as "the illusory sun about which man revolves so long as he does not revolve around himself."[26] And in the mid-nineteenth century, the self was the new, brave center contemplating an unveiled world. But one

---

[23] McLennen provides a lucid overview of the most prominent voices of post-secularity: "Manoeuvres sited towards the 'religious' end of the spectrum would include not only Charles Taylor's monumental appeal to transcendence in *A Secular Age* (2007), but also the recruitment of Michel de Certeau to the cause of radical-orthodox theology (Ward, 2000). At the secular-materialist end stands someone like Slavoj Žižek (2001, 2003), who defends the Judaeo-Christian heritage in a rather 'strategic' Leninist fashion, and theorists such as Roberto Unger (2007) and Alain Badiou (2006), who cleave firmly to atheistic and historicist tenets, but whose energized vocabularies are streaked with intimations of infinity, eternity, grace and sainthood. Somewhere in the middle of the range sit Rorty and Vattimo (2005), engaging convivially on the prospect of religion without any theists or atheists; Habermas (2008), developing grounds for dialogue between 'naturalism and religion'; and Derrida (2002) too, gesturing ever enigmatically towards 'religion without/beyond religion.'" McLennen, "The Postsecular Turn," 4.

[24] Charles Taylor, *A Secular Age* (Harvard: Harvard University Press, 2007).

[25] Luke Ferretter, *Towards a Christian Literary Theory* (Basingstoke: Palgrave, 2003). Cassandra Falke, ed. *Intersections in Christianity and Critical Theory* (Basingstoke: Palgrave, 2010).

[26] Karl Marx, "Contribution to the Critique of Hegel's Philosophy of Right, Introduction," in *The Marx-Engels Reader*, ed. Robert Tucker (New York: Norton, 1978), 54.

wonders—after Lévinas, after Asad, after Marion, dare I say, after Auschwitz, after James Byrd's murder, after the killings in Saint-Denis—have we been revolving around ourselves too long?

Marion is a Catholic theologian as well as a phenomenologist. Hans-Georg Gadamer, whose work I also draw from, is a hermeneutician, and although he was not Christian, his hermeneutic processes draw from a tradition associated with biblical criticism.[27] These men's association with Christianity makes them difficult to integrate into contemporary problems of literary theory. Literary theory has a complex relationship with philosophy in the best of discursive circumstances, and the project of bringing together phenomenology and hermeneutics with literary theory, or more boldly the work of a Christian thinker with literary theory, is bound to raise some eyebrows. Love is capacious, however. A reader who does not share Marion's belief in the source of love need not dismiss the possibility of love altogether because of that.

Hent de Vries coined the useful phrase "minimal theology" to indicate whatever it is that can be glimpsed when a critical theoretical discourse opens up a space between absolute nihilism, metaphysical absolutism, or the absolutist claims of linguistical-pragmatic constructivism.[28] Critics have reached for transcendence in a variety of forms before, alongside and in between the discourses of textuality and social constructivism.[29] The very rational idea that invisible life, God, excess, or being is only an imagined cause constructed, like a fable, by people overwhelmed by effects still posits something, a trace of something at work that is left out by that reduction to reason. Reason itself (of course) has been exposed as another construction, but there it is operating anyway. Even if one admits that the term applied to it or the boundaries of its concept are fairly arbitrary, reason keeps up its trans-personal work, as does love. Love moves people to perform a wonderful diversity of behaviors. One could easily show that the term "love" gets constructed in all sorts of ways,

[27] Textual criticism shares a general history with biblical criticism, but the word hermeneutics carries the associations much more strongly.

[28] Hent de Vries, *Minimal Theologies: Critiques of Secular Reason*, 2nd edition, trans. Geoffrey Hale (Baltimore: Johns Hopkins University Press, 2005).

[29] Regina Schwartz, e.g., lists the study of excess in aesthetics, subjectivity in psychology, and "revolutionary ecstasy" in political theory, as well as otherness in phenomenology. "Introduction," *Transcendence: Philosophy, Literature, and Theology Approach the Beyond*, ed. Regina Schwartz. (London: Routledge, 2007), vii–xi.

varying not only culture to culture, but house to house, and year to year in the life of a single individual, but regardless of how we multiply or subtract names for it, something embraced by the name of love carries on operating, oblivious to our hairsplitting.

That uncontrollable force that operates under the name of love deserves a place in the critical theoretical discussions of the future. Its absence from theoretical discussions testifies to a problem haunting literary theory in many of its manifestations, and that is the problem of theoretical acts being disconnected from the rest of our lives. Criticism should itself be an act of love. Like works of literature, works of criticism add something to the world. They enter the consciousnesses of other people in a way that, according to the logic of the erotic reduction, is unavoidably formative for a reader (however minimally). The responsibility that a critic bears for other people when she walks through town or walks into a classroom therefore also extends to her criticism. Critical theory is and must remain profoundly self-reflexive, but under the erotic reduction, the self upon which theory must reflect is plural. It extends beyond the individual critical act of a book or article and beyond the collective critical acts of one embodied person to include a vast tangle of lives that sprawls across imagined and unforeseen reading communities and the past and future loves of a critic's fragile, embodied life.

My intention in the pages that follow is not to start a new discussion about what literature might mean for our lives but rather to intervene in an ongoing conversation about why literature is valuable. Marion can offer us "counsel," to use a term from Walter Benjamin: "Counsel is less an answer to a question than a proposal concerning the continuation of a story which is just unfolding. To seek this counsel one would first have to be able to tell the story … Counsel woven into the fabric of real life is wisdom."[30] In parts of this book, I will try to tell the story of some conversations that have already taken place about love and reading, to draw together new strands of literary theoretical research with ideas from a different, more abstractly philosophical conversation about the place of love in life. I think this book's most significant contribution will be to

---

[30] Walter Benjamin, *Illuminations*, trans. Harry Zohn (New York: Schoken, 1969), 86.

welcome Marion's work more fully into this conversation. His contribution of *The Erotic Phenomenon* to this unfolding story is what ties this counsel to real life. It is what can offer wisdom. The fact that this is not a new story, but a very old one, leads me to hope that the counsel passed on in the following pages will spread into other conversations inside and outside the academy. As James Baldwin puts it "Sonny's Blues" (itself a contribution to the discussion of art and love), "while the tale of how we suffer, and how we are delighted, and how we may triumph is never new, it always must be heard. There isn't any other tale to tell, it's the only light we've got in all this darkness."[31]

---

[31] James Baldwin, "Sonny's Blues," in *The Oxford Book of American Short Stories*, ed. Joyce Carol Oates (Oxford: Oxford University Press, 1992), 438.

1

Phenomenology and Literature

Phenomenology aims to describe the ways that we experience objects and concepts, laying aside the idea that the subjectivity through which we perceive them is divisible from the objective world "out there." Phenomena are what we experience, and the subject/object division is only one possible conclusion about how phenomena reach us. Phenomenology asks: "How is it that experiences actually appear to me?" and "What is the 'me' that perceives?" For example, if I hear church bells pealing across a city, I assume that someone, somewhere is ringing them, but all I really know is the experience of the sound. I put that experience together with other phenomena of my past—the unremembered recognition of cause and effect, the sight of the church tower that morning, a conversation wherein I learned that these bells (the bells of York Minster) are still rung by hand. Each of these memories, whether or not I can consciously recollect them, also contributes to the phenomenality of hearing Minster bells. In order to describe how we experience an event such as hearing these bells, phenomenologists examine memory, the experience of selfhood, the body through which we receive sound and other sensual phenomena, our engagement with other people, and the processes by which we let an experience in or find it blocked by other experiences.[1] Phenomenologists seek rigorous ways of understanding the interrelationships among the self, the world, and the other without importing the assumption that self, world,

---

[1] Two useful introductions to phenomenology are Michael Lewis and Tanja Staehler, *Phenomenology* (London: Continuum, 2010); and Dermot Moran, *Introduction to Phenomenology* (London: Routledge, 2000). Also helpful is the more conceptually focused work by Robert Sokolowski, *Introduction to Phenomenology* (Cambridge: Cambridge University Press, 1999).

and other maintain any ontological separateness. The goal of phenomenology is not to perpetuate a philosophical debate, but to wake us up to the world. "Consciousness," writes French phenomenologist Maurice Merleau-Ponty, "must be faced with its own unreflective life in things and awakened to its own history which it was forgetting."[2]

The act of reading literature lends itself readily to phenomenological reflection. In Dermot Moran's useful phrase, phenomenology describes "world-constituting consciousness."[3] But this phrase—"world-creating consciousness"—might almost have been penned to describe what we do while reading literature. The consciousness that bodies forth memories while listening to Minster bells resembles in many ways the consciousness of a reader. The listener has more freedom to meander in thought and fewer suggestions to build on, but like the reader, she floats between perception, creation, and an enhanced awareness of the relationship between the two. Reading invokes sensual experiences and emotions that are more than memory as they recompose themselves in the spell of a text. Under the spell of a lyric poem, we share the consciousness of a speaker beholding another world. Under the spell of a novel, the world thus beheld opens itself even more fully to us in an act of "world-constituting consciousness."

In "The Origin of the Work of Art," Heidegger ascribes "world-constituting," not to phenomenology, but to art itself: "Towering up within itself, the work opens up a world and keeps it abidingly in force."[4] Phenomenology, like the literary and visual arts, increases our awareness of the actions our minds perform in relation to the world because both the phenomenologist and the artist see how inseparable mind and world are. Whereas phenomenology focuses on describing these actions, literature evokes them; it keeps our world "in force." A phenomenology of literature, then, will be a description of the ways in which literature does this, couched implicitly in the idea that it is both inevitable and good for the world to retain its force over us. What attending to

---

[2] Maurice Merleau-Ponty, *Phenomenology of Perception*, trans. Colin Smith (London: Routledge, 2002), 36.
[3] Dermot Moran, "Editor's Introduction," *The Phenomenology Reader* (London: Routledge, 2002), 1–26.
[4] Martin Heidegger, "The Origin of the Work of Art," *Basic Writings*, trans. Albert Hofstadter and ed. David Farrell Krell (London: Routledge, 1993).

the sound of bells and reading have in common is not the way they help us to escape the world, but the way they give the world back to us.

In 1919, six years after Husserl published his *Ideas: General Introduction to Pure Phenomenology*, Virginia Woolf wrote that the "the chief task of the novelist" is to "convey" how everyday the mind "receives upon its surface a myriad impressions—trivial, fantastic, evanescent, or engraved with the sharpness of steel." These impressions compose "in their sum what we might venture to call life itself; and to figure further as the semi-transparent envelope, or luminous halo, surrounding us from the beginning of consciousness to the end."[5] Woolf describes the novelist's task in terms that clarify the goal of phenomenology itself. Phenomenology seeks to describe the manner in which we receive the impressions she celebrates. The manner of attention that we turn to these impressions contains already "an infinite wealth of insight-rooted knowledge of the highest scientific worth," according to Husserl.[6] The goal of phenomenological approaches to literature, then, has been to portray the insight-rooted knowledge that becomes accessible when we turn our attention to literature. This insight changes, indeed we change, as the "luminous halo" of life is refracted and enhanced by literature. Consequently, a phenomenal description of our engagement with a single work could potentially go on forever. The description would not exhaust the insight any more than a description of light on water would exhaust the phenomenon itself.

Because the practice of looking phenomenologically at anything resembles in some ways the artistic practices of both reading and writing, it is not surprising that phenomenology and literature have a long, sometimes secret historical relationship. Literary theorists sought to describe reading/viewing/hearing literature as a phenomenon long before the terminology of phenomenology as such became available. Conversely, phenomenologists have privileged literature as a site of phenomenological description. This chapter provides an overview of the relationship between phenomenology

---

[5] Virginia Woolf, "Modern Novels," in *The Essays of Virginia Woolf*, ed. Andrew McNeillie, 6 vols. (London: Hogarth Press, 1986), 33.

[6] Edmund Husserl, *Ideas: General Introduction to Pure Phenomenology*, trans. Dermot Moran (London: Routledge, 2012), 108–109.

and literature. I begin with the reflections on art, and particularly literature, made by major thinkers within the phenomenological tradition in philosophy. This overview also contains the definition of some phenomenological terms that are likely not familiar to readers without a background in the reading of phenomenology. Following this, I provide an overview of literary criticism that has identified itself as phenomenological. Much of this criticism was written in the 1970s, but a new generation of phenomenological literary critics is already emerging. The family metaphor of "generation" implies more connectedness among younger critics than can really yet be traced. However, the history of the phenomenology of literature has some parallels with the history of continental philosophy itself in that the older emphasis on language and structure has given way to a focus on immanence and singularity.

The rich history of the interchange between phenomenology and literature has been somewhat overshadowed by a focus on literary theory grounded in categorical metaphysics (be it linguistic categorical analysis or the use of identity categories), so a revival of some phenomenological ideas regarding literature is worthwhile in itself. Reviewing the history of phenomenology and literature also clarifies what is new about the new insights that Marion's erotic reduction helps to create. Marion's writing on love provides new impetus for phenomenological ways of reading by re-grounding, rather than replacing, earlier work. I will allude to some pre-twentieth-century thinkers, but most of this chapter focuses on the phenomenological heritage of literary theory that explicitly traces its roots to Husserl. An exhaustive history of this heritage would require a volume all of its own. What follows is only a sketch.

The prehistory of phenomenology and literature

The phenomenon of perceiving a work of literature has been a focus of literary theory since Aristotle, whose definition of tragedy is based partially on a play's formal characteristics and partially on the reception of the play by the audience. Aristotle expects that a tragedy will be constructed as a unity containing a beginning, a middle, and an end and that throughout it will be "embellished" with "artistic ornament." These expectations relate to the formal elements of tragedy. However, the more dominant elements of his definition relate to the audience's perception of the play's theme as "serious" and "of a certain magnitude." According to Aristotle, viewers leave a successful tragedy having experienced a catharsis of "pity and fear," emotions that bridge the fictional world and the everyday world of the audience and that thereby point to a shared givenness of human experience that allows us to feel for characters very different than ourselves.[7] The pleasures that Aristotle assumes derive from tragedy arise from the unfolding experience of literature—an experience that incorporates the language (embellished) and structure of the play (beginning, middle, end), the past of the individual viewer, the collective response of the rest of the audience, and the emotional and intellectual engagement that the play elicits from the viewer as it unfolds in a specific temporally organized manner. Although the principles of phenomenology as such would not be developed until the early twentieth century, authors and critics since Aristotle have discussed the experience of literature as an event and an event that changes us in unpredictable ways, and this is the mystery that has fascinated critics who use the language of phenomenology itself.

To find the sources of phenomenological language, we have to jump forward to the eighteenth century where the German phrase *phänomenologisch Denkungsart*, or a phenomenological manner of thought, is used by Christoph Friedrich Oetinger. He describes phenomenological thinking as resisting the mechanistic use of categories.[8] Subsequently, *Phänomenologia*, as a noun, begins to be used in empirical philosophy to describe the philosophical investigation of appearances, which is the Latin root of the term.[9] Kant uses the term in keeping with its use by empiricists to distinguish "phenomena," or appearances, from "noumena," or essences. For Hegel, *The Phenomenology of Spirit* refers to a historical unfolding of mind or spirit through an imagined collective consciousness of this unfolding. These uses of the term, while part of the etymological history, barely foreshadow

---

[7] Aristotle, *Poetics*, trans. Stephen Halliwell (Cambridge, MA: Harvard University Press, 1995) Book 6, 1449 b27.

[8] Herbert Spiegelberg and Erwin Speigelberg, *The Phenomenological Movement: A Historical Introduction* (Dordrecht: Kluwer, 1981).

[9] "Phenomenology" in *Oxford English Dictionary*, 3rd edition, online. Also Leonard Lowlar, "Phenomenology," in *Columbia Companion to Twentieth-Century Philosophies*, ed. Constantin V. Boundas (New York: Columbia University Press, 2009), 389.

the twentieth-century usage of the term as developed by Husserl, who is generally accepted as the father of phenomenology.

The earliest recognition of an alignment between art and phenomenology as such is made by Husserl, and this seems the best place to start. Husserl suggests in his 1907 letter to Hugo Von Hofmannsthal that art, like phenomenology, invites us to set aside the "natural stance of mind" in which "Things … stand before us in a sensual way." He implies that all forms of art have this ability, but he refers specifically to an example of literary art.[10] Outside of an aesthetic or phenomenological gaze things "are posited by us as realities, and acts of mind and will are based on these positings of existence: joy—that this *is*, sorrow, that this is *not*, wish, that it could *be*, etc." Husserl here suggests that we normally struggle to engage the things of the world without imposing on them our own desire. An ontological view of that which is, is not, or could be becomes too easily entangled with an ideal projection of how we desire them to be. Husserl harkens back to Kant in implying that desire is incompatible with an aesthetic view. He feels that the aesthetic gaze, here aligned with the phenomenological gaze, escapes desire and suggests that the aesthetic and phenomenological gazes can also be epistemological. He writes, "The artist who 'observes' the world in order to gain 'knowledge' of nature and men for his own purpose relates to it in a similar way to the phenomenologist." Marion, like Husserl, seems to accept the nearness of the artist's and the phenomenologist's view. However, unlike Husserl, Marion separates the phenomenological reduction from both ontology and epistemology. He replaces both of these reductions, as already mentioned, with the phenomenologically articulated erotic reduction.

By the time Husserl penned this letter, he had already begun defining the practice of phenomenology. He wrestled with questions about the phenomenological method from the publication of his *Logical Investigations* in 1900 until his death in 1938, and it has been taken up, refined, and contested since then. In *Logical Investigations*, he expresses his frustration with both

---

[10] Edmund Husserl, "Letter to Hofmannsthal," trans. Sven-Olov Wallenstein, *Site*, 27–29 (2009), 2. He seems to be referring here to *Kleine Dramen*, a play by Hofmannsthal. My thanks to Kevin Hart for alerting me to this letter, which he also mentions in "It/Is True," *Studia Phaenomenologica* 8 (2008), 219–239.

psychologism (an empirical investigation of consciousness) and formal logic (made up of ideal structures) as inadequate in themselves and incompatible with each other.[11] Rather than focus on empirical objects being perceived or the logical structures to which objects are eventually accommodated, Husserl focused on the act of perceiving itself. By the time he published his *Ideas* in 1913, he felt that a disastrous break had occurred between the clean and predictable way that scientists and philosophers discussed the world and the actual, overwhelming, mixed-up experience of our everyday lives. In order to discuss the phenomena of life in the world, Husserl developed the concepts of intention and intuition. These concepts and the lines of inquiry Husserl develops through them became the basis of phenomenology as a definable philosophical practice.

The notion of intention had originally been proposed by one of Husserl's teachers, Franz Brentano, but in Husserl's work intentionality becomes a fundamental part of a thorough and unified introduction to a phenomenological way of thinking. In the phenomenological use of the term, when we "intend" something, we direct our attention to it—be it an object, event, or concept. We intend objects that are sensually perceivable, such as a glass of water thoughtfully left for us, but we also intend through memory things that we have seen before. I can intend a spot on a river, for example, where I swam as a child. We can intend things that we have never seen but can imagine—foreign rivers that we have only heard described to us. We can even intend concepts that we could never perceive, such as the Atlantic Ocean, or all the rain that falls one night. Looking at the ocean from an airplane, I can see one part of it. Phenomenologists call that part that shows itself to be "intuition." In its phenomenological use, the term "intention" carries no implication of future action as it does in common speech (as in "I intend to go home early tonight"), and "intuition" does not suggest a kind of sixth sense ("Intuition told me you would come").

Using the concepts of intention and intuition, Husserl devotes himself to expounding on "the absolutely independent realm of direct experience," which could only be thought about after a rejection of the "natural

---

[11] Dan Zahavi, *Husserl's Phenomenology* (Stanford: Stanford University Press, 2003), 8–10.

attitude."[12] In the natural attitude, the world of things is there for me as though it were conceptually ready-made. I take in elements of that world that seem to have qualities such as beauty or disagreeableness already stuck to them, and do what I want with them. But I give little thought to how the world reaches me. When I "bracket" the natural attitude, I set aside latent theories about the concepts or things I perceive in the world and restrict myself to trying to understand the experience of these things as it is actually given. This turning away from the natural attitude to the intuition of the things themselves is referred to as the phenomenological "reduction."[13]

The reduction can never be fully accomplished, and even in the process of taking in an everyday experience, a phenomenologically committed thinker will find the natural attitude intruding. For one thing, the timing of the reduction is complicated. If I see a green apple on a white plate, I immediately respond with ready-made concepts—food, pretty, mother's, etcetera. If I am a pomologist, the conceptual apparatus will proliferate with the names of apples, themselves so sweet on the tongue—Alderman, Dog's Snout, Granny Smith. I cannot choose to forget these ways of perceiving the apple before I see it. Any attempt to undo them after seeing the apple will involve isolating them as concepts in order to set them aside. As I do so, I am getting farther away from the moment in which I first experienced the apple, and it is the event of that experience that constitutes the phenomenon, not the apple itself as object. The moment of seeing the apple requires my presence and my intentionality as much as the presence of the apple. Once the uniqueness of my perceptive act is removed from my memory of the apple, the experience will flatten itself into a concept that resembles other similar moments that I have had or heard about. The apple sheds the halo, as Woolf called it, of thoughts, smells, hunger and beauty, out of which it emerged.

Another difficulty of remaining in the reduction is that I am faced with an apple and have only language, the memory of my body, and the sight/smell

---

[12] Edmund Husserl, "Preface to the English Edition," in *Ideas: General Introduction to Pure Phenomenology* (London: Routledge, 2002), xxxiv.

[13] The relationship between the act of bracketing the natural attitude, referred to as the "epoché," and the reduction has given rise to a number of debates within phenomenology. For an overview of this disputed relationship in Husserl, see Søren Overgaard, "Epoché and Solipsistic Reduction," *Husserl Studies* 18 (2002), 209–222.

reflection of my mind to work with. These tools are not adequate to apples, even though it is only their presence that makes the consideration of apples both possible and worthwhile. The pomologist's description of the apple will be more accurate if by accurate I mean that someone absent (another pomologist) will be able to imagine the apple's physical characteristics more precisely. But the categorical description of the apple obscures the experience of having seen the apple by claiming to have captured it. This apple—whose smell is affected by the temperature of the room, whose spots fade at the bottom, whose stem still holds a wrinkly leaf—this particular apple has vanished. In trying to recapture it in a written description, I have only language, and language falls short. Language knows only categories of apples. There is much to be said about the body's role in perceiving apples, the action of reflection, and memories of other apples, but it is language's role in the phenomenological reduction that bears most significantly on the consideration of literature. Authors have only the black-and-white marks of words to work with. When Evelyn Waugh describes Sebastian Flyte eating strawberries (to vary the example somewhat), the text itself has no memory, no sense, no action of reflection with which to engage. It must engage those things in us. As obvious as that statement may seem, the text's ability, in the case of *Brideshead Revisited*, to conjure strawberries, and longing, and a character whose degeneration we will mourn remains quite miraculous.

To understand the process by which this happens in phenomenological terms, we must return to the concept of intentionality. When I direct my attention to page thirty-two of *Brideshead Revisited*, the page on which Sebastian and Charles eat strawberries under a tree, my intention already bears the mark of my prior readings of the novel.[14] Just as I cannot un-see the greenness of an apple on a white plate, I cannot unread my first encounter with these gentlemen and their strawberries. That first reading was itself marked by a brief and lovely sojourn in Oxford, which was just the right experience out of which to construct a nostalgic longing for fictional strawberries. These prior experiences structure the intention with which

---

[14] Evelyn Waugh, *Brideshead Revisited: The Sacred and Profane Memories of Captain Charles Ryder* (London: Chapman and Hall, 1972).

I regard each page. These experiences form part of what Hans-George Gadamer calls my "horizon of meaning." My horizon includes everything within my philosophical view—beliefs that I have inherited, insights gleaned from experience, and realizations that I have arrived at through reasoned contemplation. It also includes the ways my body knows things and helps me to imagine sensual experience.[15]

In many ways, the shape of my horizon will not be visible to me until an encounter with something from outside it exposes the boundary to me. I realize, for example, that the scene where Charles and Sebastian eat strawberries has greater significance for me—it actually conveys more meaning—than the scene where Sebastian meets his nanny. I just do not have the experiential and emotional reservoir to draw from in order to understand what it is like to have a nanny. Recognizing this limitation in my reading, I realize the extent to which my experience of a nuclear family impedes my view of life in other family structures. Without us being aware of it, our horizons change so constantly that to speak of them as stable is an abstraction. As Gadamer writes, "The historical movement of human life consists in the fact that it is never absolutely bound to any one standpoint, and hence can never have a truly closed horizon."[16] But, contemplating the limitations of our own horizon expands the intention with which we face the book.

Along with my horizon, the goal with which I open the book also affects intention. Perhaps I am looking for a quotation, or I am trying to recalibrate the rhythm of my own sentences, or I am immersed in a long reading session, or I am evaluating fonts. Perhaps I have not articulated to myself a reason for opening the book at all. My intention can swerve from the novel as a whole to one passage to the act of reading itself. Intention, then, already bears the mark of prior reading experience, prior experience in the flesh, and the goal or mindset with which I approach a given page. These things structure the questions I ask of the text and the hierarchies through which I perceive different details as important. In the temporal process of reading the book, my

---

[15] Hans-George Gadamer, *Truth and Method*, trans. Joel Weinsheimer and Donald G. Marshall (London: Bloomsbury, 2013), 313.
[16] Gadamer, *Truth and Method*, 315.

intention is itself constantly changing, but part of what reading will teach me is how intention changes. The act of reading enables a reader "to clarify the conditions in which understanding takes place."[17]

Much phenomenological investigation concerns itself with the interplay between intentionality and intuition, often focusing on the poverty of what gives itself as intuition. We turn our attention to an event that happened years ago in a landscape we have just returned to only to find the memory that we can muster is incomplete. We approach a tomato glowing with color on one side and find it blighted on the other. The tomato we intended presented itself as healthy in its initial intuition, but that is only because intuition is incomplete. We could not see the whole tomato. Marion is unique among phenomenologists for being fascinated with phenomena wherein intuition, the element of the phenomenon that gives itself to perception, exceeds what we intend. These phenomena dazzle, overwhelm, amaze, and astound us. He calls these "saturated phenomena," because when they occur our intention is saturated by the intuition offered. We know that there is more being given to us than what we can take in, and we are therefore reminded of our perceptual limitations.

Every work of art can present itself as a saturated phenomenon. Our interaction with art shares this trait with our interaction with other people. In each of these cases, encountering art and encountering another person, the experience of a saturated phenomenon is a possibility rather than a guarantee. A work of literature or a painting may appear to us as what Marion calls a "common-law" phenomenon. These are phenomena wherein we receive the intuition offered to us just enough to match a limited amount of attention that we pay to something we need to make use of and move on from it. I could admire a coffee cup, but very often I do not. I grab the nearest, fill it up, and move on. My limited, efficient intention restricts the intuition that the cup offers me, so that unless some delicacy of the cup startles me into greater attention, my intentionality remains unsaturated. Literature can be approached this way, also. It can fit our argument, mood, or desire for entertainment just so, but if we let ourselves be satisfied with that we have missed an opportunity. Art does not readily comply with our expectations. We damage it to make it fit.

[17] Gadamer, *Truth and Method*, 306.

Marion celebrates the fact that we will frequently find more phenomenality granted to us than we can possibly take in. He uses the concept to explore our engagement with specific classes of phenomena following "the guiding thread of Kantian categories"—quantity, quality, modality, and relation. He discusses these as four kinds of experience and describes the ways in which they saturate our intention. First, the event overwhelms us according to quantity; it is too much to take in as it unfolds, too great to have anticipated beforehand, and too full of detail to adequately recall later. The hermeneutic required by the event is also unquantifiable, offering a "surplus of effects . . . over every system of causes" and a surplus of interpretations.[18] Second, painting is discussed as "an idol" "that the look cannot bear." A painting, viewed as an idol, saturates the gaze according to quality. In a painting, we encounter "a reduced visible, presented in the pure state without any remainder of appresentation"—no far side of a pictured mountain, no face if a painted head is turned away. This "pure visible . . . reaches such an intensity that it often saturates the capacity of my look" and thereby "defines what I can bear of phenomenality."[19] In this way, the painting as idol serves as a mirror reflecting the viewer's own capacity. In contrast to the idol, the icon, which exceeds intention according to modality, functions as a window. The icon confronts us with the face of another. That face opposes me with a signification and intentionality that imposes itself on me without concept, and therefore represents "the saturated phenomenon par excellence."[20] Finally, Marion describes the flesh as saturated according to relation. The flesh is unique with regard to other saturated phenomena because whereas they "designate each time what the *ego* cannot constitute as its object," the flesh "delivers the *ego* to itself."[21] In all these cases, by shattering the conceptual framework that we try to apply to them, saturated phenomena startle and permanently change us. Merleau-Ponty says that phenomenology's initiating act is "wonder in the face of the world,"[22] and we might say that the founding act of a phenomenology of literature is wonder, too.

[18] Marion, *In Excess*, 36, 33.
[19] Marion, *In Excess*, 63, 61.
[20] Marion, *In Excess*, 126.
[21] Marion, *In Excess*, 100, italics in original.
[22] Merleau-Ponty, *Phenomenology of Perception*, xiii.

Literature and wonder

The more recent historical relationship between phenomenology and literary theory is erratic and hard to trace. In *The Glossary of Literary Terms* from 1999, M. H. Abrams, with magisterial clarity, mentions Gadamer (1900–2002) as the first to use phenomenology to understand the actions performed when reading literature.[23] He goes on to mention Polish critic Roman Ingarden (1893–1970), whose work in the 1930s influenced German critics Wolfgang Iser (1926–2007) and Hans-Robert Jauss (1921–1997). He discusses the Geneva School scholars, who identified themselves as phenomenological critics explicitly. This group included Georges Poulet (1902–1991), Marcel Raymond (1897–1981), Albert Béguin (1901–1957), Jean Starobinski (1920–), and Jean-Pierre Richard (1922–). Were Abrams's entry to be rewritten today, it would need also to accommodate the work of Paul Ricoeur (1913–2005), whose focus on phenomenology and hermeneutics deals with recurring questions of narrativity, mimesis, the responsibilities of literary criticism and literature's relation to the self. It would probably include the work of Gaston Bachelard (1884–1962) who calls poetry "the phenomenology of the soul,"[24] and whose work on space and reverie are increasingly cited in literary analysis. Perhaps the story of phenomenology and literature should also take Bachelard at his word and discuss the phenomenology performed by poets and novelists to whom the language of phenomenology was not yet available. As François Cusset notes, contemporary phenomenological critics of literature are more likely to quote literary writers on reading than they are to quote phenomenologists per se.[25]

A new entry would need, finally, to account for the rediscovery of phenomenology occurring in literary criticism now. Rita Felski deserves to be placed near the head of the scholars now turning back to phenomenology. Although she practices, in her own words, "at best an impure or hybrid phenomenology" herself, her leadership of *New Literary History* has provided

---

[23] M. H. Abrams, "Phenomenology and Criticism," in *A Glossary of Literary Terms*. 7th edition (Boston: Heinle and Heinle, 1999), 220–223.

[24] Gaston Bachelard, *The Poetics of Space*, trans. Maria Jolas (Boston: Beacon, 1994), xxi.

[25] François Cusset, "Unthinkable Readers: The Political Blindspot of French Literature," *New Literary History* 44 (2013): 260–261.

a visible venue for scholars who claim phenomenology more directly. Felski suggests that in her new "hybrid" phenomenology "everyday attitudes are neither invalidated (as they are in post-structuralism and much political criticism) nor are they taken as self-explanatory (as in humanist criticism with its unexamined use of terms such as 'self' or 'value'), rather they become worthy of investigation in all their many-sidedness."[26] This characterization of the new phenomenological criticism's relationship to everyday life captures the spirit with which most of its practitioners are returning to Husserl and Heidegger and discovering Marion. Kevin Hart has also contributed significantly to phenomenological literary criticism, not only through his reviews and articles exemplifying a phenomenological method, but also through his work mediating between phenomenology and literature. As the editor of Marion's *Essential Writings* and an important collection of essays about the philosopher, Hart has made Marion's ideas more accessible to literary critics.

Abrams's goal in his *Glossary* was to provide an overview of the history of phenomenological criticism as a documentation of a stage in critical history. My goal here is to revive previous insights of phenomenological critics that are useful for the contemplation of love and reading. So, rather than providing a chronological overview organized around central figures, I provide an overview organized around major themes of phenomenological criticism. These are all areas where research could move forward. Returning to scholarship from the 1970s may not be fashionable, but the habit of building only on recent criticism presumes one of two beliefs about scholarship: a Hegelian movement toward perfection or a scientific model where new scholarship resembles new discoveries that replace outdated knowledge. Neither of these beliefs seems a very viable basis for the current project. If we imagine, instead, criticism as a conversation, then it makes sense to link new thoughts with the conversation going on at present, but it can also be valuable to invoke previous conversations where wisdom was learned and forgotten.

One theme of previous phenomenological literary criticism that will be particularly important for considering the erotic reduction is the similarity between the apparent consciousness of a book and the consciousness of

---

[26] Felski, *The Uses of Literature*, 16–17.

another embodied person. In his 1969 essay, "The Phenomenology of Reading," Georges Poulet describes the startling awareness we feel when opening a book:

> I realize that what I hold in my hands is no longer just an object, or even simply a living thing. I am aware of a rational being, of a consciousness; the consciousness of another, no different from the one I automatically assume in every human being I encounter, except that in this case the consciousness is open to me, welcomes me, lets me look deep inside itself, and even allows me, with unheard-of license, to think what it thinks and feel what it feels.[27]

Poulet stresses that inside a reader's mind a book becomes "a mind conscious of itself and constituting itself as the subject of its own object."[28] Each work of literature instructs us how to read it by becoming "the subject of its own object." To paraphrase Wordsworth, it creates the taste by which it will be enjoyed during the process of reading. For Poulet, this is evidence of a book's similarity to an encounter with the other, but he presumes quite an idealized encounter with another subjectivity in order to make this claim. To engage another person as the subject of his own object would be to see him as he sees himself. Although it may be the ideal of several moral systems for us to do unto others as we would have them do unto us, or to see others as they would have us see them, this ideal is not always easy to attain with other people in the flesh. Such action and such vision requires love for and foreknowledge of the other person.

If novels and poems act on us in a way that better enables us to recognize the manner in which another consciousness desires to be seen, then that is a very good reason to read them. Marion describes a moment in our love for another in which we feel ourselves constituted by the intentionality of the beloved other. We become the object of their subjectivity, to use Poulet's language, and it topples our sense of control and autonomy. We become visible within the erotic reduction because of the other seeing us (*EP* 80). Conversely, as lovers, we grant visibility to the other by seeing our beloved and by seeing him or her as lovable. If a book has the ability to pull away our autonomy and

---

[27] Georges Poulet, "The Phenomenology of Reading," *New Literary History* 1:1 (October 1969): 54.
[28] Poulet, "Phenomenology of Reading," 59.

replace our way of seeing it with the way of seeing that will bring it most into visibility, then this is a practice worth learning as a lover.

Poulet also assumes quite an immersive reading experience wherein the book's consciousness "suspends" the life of the human reader. Many readers probably do not remain so immersed that their life is suspended during an entire reading session. Life reasserts itself. But it is easy to imagine a spectrum of reading immersion with Poulet's total suspension of the reader's own consciousness at one end of it. He recognizes that any single critic will occupy a variety of positions in relation to a reading, sometimes letting herself be overcome by a book's subjectivity and sometimes viewing it as object, but he worries that this dialectical process will leave the critic "oscillat[ing] between two possibilities: a union without comprehension and a comprehension without union." Both of these miss "that mysterious interrelationship" of text and reader that constitutes the phenomenon of a "total critical act."[29] He notes three critics from his own time who performed their work at different points along this imaginary spectrum of immersion and who tried to find ways of speaking about the interrelationship of text and reader by working within the phenomenological reduction. The critic whose work he praises the most, Jean Rousset, attends to the tension between a work's "will to stability" and "its protean impulse," and this might be a model for engaging a work of literature in a way that attends to its real autonomy from the critic while also allowing it to give the reader its own way of seeing itself.

A work's stable features set boundaries on the protean impulse that a reader's relation to a text enables. Focusing on this tension between what gives itself, stably, in a text, and what we receive, which is affected by the protean possibilities of a text, privileges the relationship between text and reader in a way that a focus on the patterns of a text alone cannot. As something given, with its own rhythm, its own artistic palette, a work of literature has a kind of will of its own. Poulet calls it consciousness. Reflection shows that although this may at first seem correct, the book is not quite conscious because it resists us more than the malleable consciousness of another person does.

---

[29] Poulet, "Phenomenology of Reading," 63.

Nevertheless, a book's initial resemblance to a speaking consciousness does account for its unpredictable ability to alter the way we see things.

Another theme that has recurred in phenomenological criticism has been temporality. As Ricoeur puts it, "the temporal quality of experience" forms a "common reference of both history and fiction." History here is not limited to the grand sweep of national and international events, but includes all the forms of historical storytelling such as the story we tell ourselves about our own past.[30] The unfolding of a story or poem occurs as an event in time, just as the recollection of our own past does or the story someone else tells us. For phenomenological critics, a text is never treated as something that could be removed from the time-bound event of reading. All objects reach us as events. Husserl writes that in everyday experience "every step forward yields new points of view from which what we have already discovered appears in a new light, so that often enough what we were originally able to take as simple and undivided presents itself as complex and full of distinction."[31] When applied to literature, this insight suggests what Roman Ingarden called "intentional sentence correlatives," the expectation that each sentence arouses. We might also describe "intentional image correlatives" or "intentional character correlatives." The sentence is only one of the units of a text that arouses expectations.

As Wolfgang Iser explains the general concept, the sentences in literary texts often create expectations that are not fulfilled, and our expectation becomes the expectation of surprise itself. Each

> intentional sentence correlative opens up a particular horizon, which is modified, if not completely changed, by succeeding sentences. While these expectations arouse interest in what is to come, the subsequent modification of them will also have a retrospective effect on what has already been read.[32]

One remarkable trait of this present-tense revision of the past in literature is that we often do not notice how our perception of the foregoing text is

---

[30] Ricoeur, *From Text to Action: Essays in Hermeneutics, II*, 2.

[31] Edmund Husserl, *On Phantasy, Image, Consciousness and Memory*, trans. John B. Brough, *Collected Works*, Vol. II (Dordrecht: Springer, 2005), 19.

[32] Wolfgang Iser, "The Reading Process: A Phenomenological Approach," *New Literary History* 3:2 (Winter 1972): 283. See also Iser, *The Act of Reading: A Theory of Aesthetic Response* (Baltimore: Johns Hopkins, 1978), 148–150.

changing. Because as readers we do not bear the responsibility of deciding what to do, say, or think next in a text, we often do not look into our memory of the text unless the text itself prompts us to do so. If a character has been hidden from view and suddenly reappears, then we may try to recall details about him or her. If the structure recalls an earlier incident (a parallel scene to one that occurred earlier, a clue that places a character at the scene of a crime based on information we already have), then we may note both the earlier incident and the literary formulation that drew our attention to it. But however little attention we pay to the text's past, we must carry that past with us in the reading-present in order for the new sentences we encounter to be meaningful.

All sorts of nuances of the text's past are activated as we move forward in a text. When Huckleberry Finn discovers Jim on Jackson's Island, we read: "Pretty soon he gapped and stretched himself and hove off the blanket, and it was Miss Watson's Jim! I bet I was glad to see him." On a rudimentary level, "he" only makes sense in light of the previous sentence wherein Huck sees a man lying by a fire. "Miss Watson's Jim" only makes sense if we recall encountering Jim, Miss Watson, and the slave/slave-owner relationship before. "Hove off the blanket" draws in our familiarity with Huck's way of speaking and the assumptions we have about people who use his dialect. Moreover the action-packed series of "gapped" and "stretched" and "hove" only seems action-packed in light of Huck's patient, still, minutely described waiting, which precedes it. "I bet I was glad to see him" resolves the tension of the previous paragraph only because the recollection of that tension is still latently present as we read this last sentence. As this example illustrates, a single "intentional sentence correlate" contains expectations about the objects or persons to which words refer, the dialogism of type of speech, the pacing of action and the mood. Most sentences do not repay mining them for all of our expectations. New adventures are calling in sentences soon to come, so readers generally move within an intentionality shaped by the past of the text without being aware of expectations at all. Nevertheless, it is hard not to sense a text overflowing our expectations as we move forward. The temporal sense of moving forward becomes conditioned by the expectation of this overabundance, and that drives the reading. Temporal awareness therefore becomes a condition of our pleasure in and our understanding of a text.

This temporal awareness stretches beyond the bounds of the text. My reaction to Huck's use of the word "hove" will be conditioned by my prior experience with the word and the people I have known to use it. The level of relief I feel when Huck recognizes Jim will be conditioned by the peace I have felt in real woods and the effect that the sudden discovery of someone else's presence has had on that peace. Someone who has not known that peace or had it disturbed will react less strongly. When the associations borrowed from our reading-past and the past beyond a book accumulate, certain fictional moments achieve a density that renders them more important for an individual reading of a text than the structure of the text conceived objectively might justify. Alberto Manguel recalls a moment in *Alice in Wonderland* that for him contains "an experience of" and perhaps even "a philosophy of" life itself. Alice has passed through the chessboard fields that met her on the far side of the looking-glass and come to a dark wood. In the wood, nothing has a name. Having been too warm in the fields, Alice says to herself, "'I mean to get under the—under the—under the *this*, you know!' putting her hand on the trunk of a tree. 'What does it call itself, I wonder? I do believe it's got no name. Why to be sure it hasn't.'" Manguel goes on to speculate about the nature of language, ontology, and Adam.[33] Alice's moment in the wood exerts a kind of gravitational pull, drawing other reading experiences and life-born insights into the moment of reading. The density of that moment in the reading experience he describes derives in part, but only in part, from the quality of Carroll's idea and the presentation of it in the novel.

There is a moment that has as much weight for me as Alice's crisis of naming has for Manguel. In *Absalom! Absalom!* Shreve, Quentin Compson's Canadian roommate at Harvard, pontificates that Southerners outlive themselves for years and years.[34] So, as readers, do we all. Whereas our time-consciousness is bound in real time by our bodily location in a specific moment, our time-consciousness as readers carries pasts we have not lived and futures that we cannot enact. But for all that, readerly time-consciousness does not exclude the past we have lived through our bodies and the future we will live in

[33] Quoted in Alberto Manguel, *A Reader in the Looking-Glass Wood: Essays on Books, Reading and the World* (San Diego: Harcourt, 1998), 12.
[34] William Faulkner, *Absalom! Absalom!* (New York: Modern Library, 2012), 382.

community with nonfictional others. It is our awareness of nonfictional future possibility that makes our fictional experience valuable to us as lovers.

The final theme that I wish to revive from earlier phenomenological work is the theme of the endless hermeneutic, the infinite possibility for interpreting literary texts that expands within the bounds set by the text itself. Quentin Compson always attends Harvard, never Oxford, or Old Miss, but the reading experience of his scene with shreve is always new. Questions about why Quentin attended Harvard or why he commits suicide are unresolvable. Iser writes that it "is this very inexhaustibility" of the text that forces the reader to make his interpretive decision.[35] The effort to resolve interpretive questions sends us exploring possible explanations supported both by the text and by our preconceived ideas about what could motivate an act of suicide. Once a reader reaches the point of questioning Quentin's suicide, the framework for discovering an answer is already shaped by the reason she wants to ask. Asking about a character's motivation, or the function of a specific moment in the overall structure of a work or her own reasons for wanting to know, the reader will begin a contemplation of the text and the act of reading. Such contemplation will range over the memory of the text, and what memory gives her in that moment of contemplation will itself be shaped by myriad invisible forces.

It is easy for professional scholars to follow critical convention and pretend that our recollection of a text is entirely subordinated to the demands of an argument or theoretical perspective, but asserting that level of control over scholarly reading is not only misleading (we are not machines), it is also counterproductive. It makes scholarly reading appear so different from reading for pleasure that the insights of professional readers may seem irrelevant for the majority of readers. Formulating multiple possible meanings of a text, a process called imaginative variation within phenomenology, is part of a scholar's responsibility as a teacher and researcher. Nevertheless, the endless hermeneutic is not only available to professional scholars practiced in acts of imaginative variation, but is a fact of any experience of reading literature. "Indeterminacy," as phenomenological critics call it, is a property of literary texts as such. The rise of both phenomenological criticism and

---

[35] Iser, "The Reading Process," 285.

post-structuralist theory in the 1970s brought indeterminacy to the fore of much literary theoretical discussion.

As Charles Altieri noted in 1978, three explanations of indeterminacy were much debated. In what he calls a psychological view of indeterminacy, the inability to arrive at certainty when interpreting texts arises from the complexity of individual reader reactions. We cannot say for certain why Quentin kills himself because the imagining of his mental state and social circumstances leading up to that event will vary too much from reader to reader. Altieri points out that much reader-response criticism assumes a psychological explanation for indeterminacy. The second kind of explanation for indeterminacy, he calls "logical." Logical explanations for indeterminacy hinge on language's dynamism in relation to empirical experience. When Huck describes a morning wind as "ripply," the reader may logically construe this as evoking a comparison with water, or he may imagine that the wind ripples Huck's thin clothes. The word refers with equal plausibility to both. Derrida sees logical indeterminacy as a basis for seeing all new acts of meaning-making as undermining previous ones. For him, logical indeterminacy indicates that we use a tissue of language that is through and through more connected to itself than anything else. Other critics, such as the Russian formalists, who ascribe logical indeterminacy to literary texts resist seeing this as a property of language more broadly and celebrate literature's difference from common speech on the grounds of its being able to convey a greater number of possible meanings.

Finally, Altieri refers to a thematic basis of indeterminacy. In this category, he includes critics who see literary texts as establishing tensions between multiple possibilities of meanings without the form of the text indicating which possible meaning to prioritize. Literature, in this view, comes to represent the broader difficulties of consciousness interpreting the empirical world. Quentin's suicide defies explanation because all suicides defy explanation. Huck's fortunate turn of phrase alludes to his tendency to see one form of experience (the wind blowing) in terms of another experience he values (rowing a river). This tendency, viewed in light of thematic indeterminacy, makes visible the shaping force that prior experiences have on our present ones, including the shaping force that reading *Huckleberry Finn* will have on our future perception of wind.

Altieri warns that each of these explanations for indeterminacy "reduces objectivity to discussions of physical properties and banishes all other forms of meaning to essentially individual acts."[36] Against this reductionist view, he posits the possibility of sharing "agreement among inquiries or descriptions of a phenomenon."[37] This agreement facilitates basic acts of communication all the time as well as basic acts of figuration when we read fiction or poetry. Indeterminacy arises both from the agreement about meaning making that language itself represent and the localized practices of determining meaning that shape each reader. Within the erotic reduction, agreement must be viewed as related to the networks of love. These networks include relationships between students and teachers and communities of scholars—the institutionalized interpretive communities to which many readers belong. It also includes the communities in which readers are raised—the managerial class in a mining town, an immigrant community, or a gang of inner-city bohemians. It includes webs of filiation with other readers who are, for example, extremely fond of Faulkner or nuanced reciters of Poe. The language that makes up literature comes to us "out of other people's mouths" as Bakhtin says,[38] saturated with meanings from these webs of filiation. The operation of interpretive communities of historically varying cultural norms and institutional influences have all been written about, but the webs of filiation behind them have remained invisible. These webs of filiation shape texts without eliminating their indeterminacy. The fact that prior loves give shape to a literary interpretive question does not reduce a text's hermeneutic potential, but it does partially determine the specific ways that texts function meaningfully in our lives.

The sources of indeterminacy discussed above (psychological, logical, and thematic) are all oriented toward the reception of a text, but readers are not the only active party in an encounter with literature. In a sense, a work of literature is itself an action. Its indeterminacy arises in a profound way from the fact that its action is not the action of determination. Quentin is not carved out, or

---

[36] Charles Altieri, "The Hermeneutics of Literary Indeterminacy," *New Literary History* 10, no. 1 (1978): 77.

[37] Altieri, "Hermeneutics of Literary Indeterminacy," 77.

[38] Mikail Bakhtin, *The Dialogic Imagination: Four Essays by M. M. Bakhtin*, trans. Caryl Emerson and Michael Holquist and ed. Michael Holquist (Austin: University of Texas Press, 1981), 291.

determined, from within already known possibilities of human character. He exposes possibilities of human character that are utterly unique. In Marion's view, painting makes visible what previously could not be seen and thereby adds to the visibility of the world. Kandinsky's *Houses at Murnau* makes possible the new phenomena that occur when people view it. Every new thing, every flower that grows or new building that goes up does this in a way, but Marion privileges painting because it facilitates a kind of phenomenon that could not be brought into being any other way. The same could be said for a poem, story, or novel. *Houses at Murnau, Absalom!, Absalom!,* and *Huckleberry Finn* are indeterminate because they do not set a choice to be made or a hypothesis to be proven. They do not terminate possibilities (de-termine) but illuminate them. A work of literature is like a cry. We hear it as a cry of joy, passion, or distress, but the action is precisely the action of the cry that it is. It is a cry because it cannot be a statement. Literature enables a new vision but not a determination.

New phenomenological criticism has not abandoned inquiries onto a text's pseudo-consciousness, temporality, or the endless hermeneutic a text offers, but the terms of our debates about literature have changed. Now temporality is discussed as event-ness. Pseudo-consciousness returns in discussions of inter-subjectivity, and the endless hermeneutic is taken for granted. The debate with regard to it is now whether endless interpretive possibilities are created or discovered, or the extent to which they might be falsely limited by the activity of identity categories and ideologies. Most new phenomenological criticism, whether it calls itself such or not, focuses on the actions that literature performs. Rita Felski focuses on recognition, enchantment, knowledge, and shock. Joshua Landy posits many more options because he argues that every work "contains within itself a manual for reading, a set of implicit instructions on how it may best be used." The title of his book, *How to Do Things with Fiction*, implies a reader who masters the text at hand. The approach to reading that he models through his accounts of Beckett, Plato, the Gospel of Mark, and others suggests, in contrast, a willingness to let a book set the terms by which it will be read. This receptivity of method fits very well with a view of art as saturated phenomena. It also fits well with the receptivity of a lover who lets himself be seen from elsewhere, and being seen, shifts his vision of himself. Steven Connor has been doing interesting work in what he calls "cultural phenomenology." This situates literature among other cultural discourses. Dreaming about what this non-discipline could be in 2000, he defined it as a practice of thinking in public more than a method: "Instead of readings of abstract social and psychological structures, functions and dynamics, cultural phenomenology would home in on substances, habits, organs, rituals, obsessions, pathologies, processes and patterns of feeling. Such interest would at once be philosophical and poetic, explanatory and exploratory, analytic and evocative."[39] Challenging the isolationist thinking of Husserl and Heidegger, Connor posits that new phenomenological work will acknowledge the formative role of intersubjective experience.

Different as they are, each of these three scholars challenges approaches to literature and culture that imagine critics swooping down from heights of intellect to make a sort of prey of a literary object. They embrace what Marion calls the "double modification of the reduction," the process by which our viewing is altered by what we view.[40] Coming to this sort of understanding about a text does not follow the process of experimentation by which much argument proceeds. It does not begin with a hypothesis to measure a text against. It is more like looking for mushrooms or regarding an anamorphic painting. Only a shift in perspective reveals what is hidden. In *Being and Time*, Heidegger defines logic itself according to a viewer's apophatic action of letting-something-be-seen.[41] In literary interpretation, then, a text offers its own terms for understanding, its own perspective within which it will reveal itself, and a reader's interpretation does not exert itself upon a text after that fact as much as rise up from the work itself. Understanding is already couched in interpretation. The wonder that a phenomenological critic experiences in reading is wonder at the revelation a text offers, and the critical act is an effort to display the text in a way that facilitates other readers' wonder at what the text offers them, which will be influenced by but not identical to the critic's own moment of letting the text be seen.

---

[39] Steven Connor, "Making an Issue of Cultural Phenomenology," *Critical Inquiry* 42, no. 1 (2000): 3.

[40] Jean-Luc Marion, "Concluding Lecture," *Breached Horizons Conference* (March 28, 2015), Centre for Advanced Research in European Philosophy, King's University College, London, Canada. Thanks to Antonio Calcagno for reminding me of this term.

[41] Martin Heidegger, *Being and Time*, trans. John Macquarrie and Edward Robinson (Oxford: Blackwell, 1962), 56.

One final point should be made about new phenomenological criticism and its potential to go to seed. Phenomenological critics use language that attaches criticism to the rest of our lives. Kevin Hart uses wine sedimentation to illustrate Marion's concept of the idol and discusses the phenomenology of absence by remembering his friend, Robert.[42] Connor explicitly rejects what he calls "the airline English of theorytalk."[43] When Landy writes, ostensibly about Proust, that "we no longer trust naïve, spontaneous outbursts of enthusiasm; what we trust is, instead, the passion of a cynic,"[44] I suspect he is talking about more than Proust. Critics spend time with Milton and cummings and Muldoon, who in turn spend time with angels and prostitutes and hedgehogs. If we confine our language to language that, in its abstraction, misses the texture of our fecund and multifarious life, then it is our fault. The language on the pages we pore over offers more, as does the life we live.

---

[42] Hart, *Essential Writings*, 58 and 9.
[43] Connor, "Making an Issue," 5.
[44] Landy, *How to Do Things*, 90.

2

The Erotic Reduction

As I mentioned in the introduction, the ontological and epistemic reductions can make us certain of our own being but cannot give us a reason for continuing to be. In this chapter, I discuss in detail the erotic reduction that Marion proposes as an alternative to these two and follow up with some implications the erotic reduction has for reading. We may, Marion suggests, have the Cartesian or Heideggerian realization that here we are existing, and still ask "What's the point of my existing? Why do I want to keep existing?" In order to address these questions, we have to see ourselves as connected to other beings. "In order for me to *be* not only certainly, but with a certainty that matters to me" I have to "be with a being that assures me from elsewhere" (*EP* 23). Marion's response, therefore, to Descartes' formulation "I think, therefore I am" or the phenomenological "I am aware of my own being and becoming, therefore I am" is "I love, therefore I am." I love therefore I want to continue to be. I love and am loved, or at the very least, I live in the awareness of the absence and hope of love, and therefore my being matters.

The erotic phenomenon is a process that we initiate, observe, repeat, and interrupt in an endless variety of ways with a great variety of people. Abandoned as a concept by philosophers and manipulated by individuals and corporations, "love" asserts Marion, "is the most prostituted word there is … one 'makes' love like one makes war or makes deals" (*EP* 3). "Charity," too, he contends, has lost its resonance. We do not even find it sophisticated enough to describe giving. We use instead " 'fellowship,' 'solidarity,' [and] 'humanitarian aid' " (*EP* 4). *Eros*, Marion hopes, has retained enough potency to carry the conceptual weight of the erotic reduction. Because "a serious concept of love distinguishes itself by its unity," Marion uses the words "eros" and "erotic" to describe any and all love that we experience with anyone for any period of time (*EP* 5). The loves that we experience with a spouse, lover, friend, parent, or child may differ from one another, but they are not separable categories of love. Every love is always unique. Marion's refusal to assign different names to friend-love, God-love, or spouse-love testifies to the uniqueness of our loving relationships more than to their sameness. We cannot call the love we share with all our friends, for example, by the same name, but must instead call them by the name of each friend. Even the "little, nameless, unremembered acts/ of kindness" that Wordsworth lyricizes in "A Few Lines Written Above Tintern Abbey" (lines 35–36) are erotic. We cannot recall them. We may not have an ongoing relationship with the person with whom we performed them, but loving acts become permanently part of us (*EP* 188). In all varieties of the erotic phenomenon, whether they take place between friends, in families, or with a pledged beloved, love speaks with the same voice (*EP* 217).[1]

Marion compresses several hundred years of philosophy in hopscotching from Descartes to Heidegger to himself. This makes the erotic reduction stand out clearly in opposition to philosophy's historical preoccupation with knowledge and being. It is worth remembering, however, as Marion puts it elsewhere, that "the development of phenomenology, with the massive exception of Heidegger to be sure, has aimed only at constructing a doctrine without the being of the I."[2] Within this more narrow history of phenomenology's wanderings away from being, Marion has some important precursors. Merleau-Ponty contested the autonomy of the I by drawing attention to the body's "inspired exegesis" of the world, an exegesis that does not pass through knowledge or transcendental being, but that just operates.[3] The

---

[1] For an examination of the unity of love in Marion's writing, see Beáta Tóth, "Love Between Embodiment and Spirituality: Jean-Luc Marion and John Paul II on Erotic Love," *Modern Theology* 29 (2013). Tóth suggests that Marion accomplishes a unified concept of love by reversing the historical tendency to revere spiritual, disembodied love more than love confirmed through sexual union. She worries, however, that Marion attends inadequately to love's emotional aspects and that the inclusion of more specific descriptions of love's emotion might threaten the perception of love as unified.

[2] Jean-Luc Marion, *Reduction and Givenness: Investigations of Husserl, Heidegger and Phenomenology*, trans. Thomas A. Carlson (Evanston, IL: Northwestern University Press, 1998), 239.

[3] Maurice Merleau-Ponty, *The Visible and the Invisible*, trans, Claude Lefort (Evanston: Northwestern University Press, 1968), 133.

smell of jasmine comes to me. I do not need to exert my being-ness or will to find it, nor do I need to know that it is jasmine in order to experience the smell. The experience occurs without my permission or conceptual knowledge. It is a given. Merleau-Ponty does not privilege the language of givenness as Marion does, but his explorations of the self porous to the world as given through the body and porous to other selves contests the focus on being that Heidegger left as his phenomenological legacy.

The sense of the ego's dependence becomes more radicalized in the phenomenology of Emmanuel Lévinas, whose *Otherwise than Being* directly critiques the possibility of a transcendental ego. For Lévinas, the self's "responsibility for the other, the proximity of the neighbor does not signify 'a submission to the non-ego.' It critiques ontology as such more fundamentally than this. It means an openness in which being's essence is surpassed in inspiration." Lévinas, like Marion, suggests a "self without concept."[4] One of Marion's earliest essays on love, "The Intentionality of Love," is dedicated to Lévinas, and the elder philosopher's influence on Marion's erotic reduction is clear. Marion accomplishes a further radicalization by locating otherness in the specific, local, present flesh of individual beloveds.

Two final predecessors are worth mentioning, Michel Henry and Jacques Derrida. These two philosophers have shaped Marion's thinking by providing the ideas that he honed his own against. Michel Henry develops a concept of auto-affection wherein the self finds love, particularly self-love through the immanent love of Christ. This immanence, closer than our knowledge of who we are and overflowing the illusion of objectivity, provides a truth that can ground us after the dissolution of metaphysics. Henry maintains a focus on invisible life throughout his writing, and when he writes *I Am the Truth: Toward a Philosophy of Christianity* (1996, trans. 2003), he links "the self-enjoyment of absolute life" to love, and love to God.[5] By locating action and being in love's immanence, Henry inspires a turn to love within phenomenology.

---

[4] Emmanuel Lévinas, *Otherwise than Being*, trans. Alphonso Lingis (Dordrecht: Kluwer Academic Publisher, 1981), 115.

[5] Michel Henry, *I Am the Truth: Toward a Philosophy of Christianity*, trans. Susan Emmanuel (Stanford: Stanford University Press, 2003), 31.

Participating in this turn, too, is Jacques Derrida. By the time Derrida wrote his reflection on love, *The Politics of Friendship*, he felt that phenomenology had exhausted itself. Nevertheless, phenomenology is the discourse that Derrida most frequently sees himself at the end of. In his writings on friendship and gift, Derrida defines the position that Marion argues against.[6] For Derrida, the social structures that bind friendship to utility and gift to exchange can be transmuted but never escaped. For Marion, love and gift do not arise within or contend against social structures, but give rise to them.

The conversation

Marion is perhaps best known for his conception of the saturated phenomenon, which he theorized in *Being Given* (1997: trans. 2002) and *In Excess* (2001; trans. 2002), but he insists that since 1977 all of his books, including these two, have borne "the mark" of his fixation on the erotic phenomenon. Marion understands each of us to be created solely by the love and hate we make with others. Neither the lover nor the beloved has a transcendent ego preceding the act of love (*EP* 216). Because of this foundational interdependence, it is appropriate that he describes the erotic phenomenon, not as an abstracted concept, but as an event unfolding like a conversation between two people. In the erotic phenomenon, the first step is to ask: "Does anyone out there love me?" (*EP* 22). We are driven to ask this when we realize that the ontological and epistemic reductions provide us with no purpose but only certainty. And, as Marion says, "The certainty of my existence is never enough to make it just, or good, or beautiful, or desirable" (*EP* 22). Certainty, Marion charges, was never the goal of philosophy, conceived as the love of wisdom, but of metaphysics, a "science of objects—that pottage of lentils" (*EP* 2). Marion demonstrates the weakness of the certainty provided by the ontological and epistemic reductions with two arguments, one logical, one experiential.

---

[6] Jacques Derrida, *The Politics of Friendship* (London: Verso, 2005). See also Jacques Derrida and Jean-Luc Marion, "On the Gift: A Discussion between Jacques Derrida and Jean-Luc Marion Moderated by Richard Kearney," in *God, the Gift, and Postmodernism*, ed. John Caputo and Michael J. Scanlon (Bloomington, IN: Indiana University Press, 1999).

First, he points to its circularity. "If my certainty depends on me, this very surety, that I must decide about, can in no way reassure me, since, even fully accomplished, it only has me as its origin—this me that it is in turn necessary to secure" (*EP* 18). Then, he appeals to us as experienced lovers, "Who can hold seriously that the possibility of finding oneself loved and hated does not concern him at all?" (*EP* 26).

Marion's formulation of the question "Does anyone out there love me?" is significant. Whereas the syntax of "Am I loved?" would remain focused entirely on the self, the formulation "Does anyone out there love me?" acknowledges our dependence on someone else, an alternate intentionality, "anyone." We cannot ask "Am I loved?" without positing an "I" that in fact does not exist outside of its relation with the one "out there" (*EP* 37). By emphasizing this counter-intentionality "out there," Marion reminds readers of the essential solitariness we experience in spite of love's constituting power. In *The Symposium*, Plato has Aristophanes voice the belief that "primeval man" was once cut in two like an apple for pickling, and now forever looks for the other half of himself in order to feel complete again.[7] In this imagining of love, each individual needs another person in order to fill a lack. Even though he argues that we are not ourselves adequate for selfhood without our beloveds, Marion does not suggest that we have a lack needing to be filled by a particular individual or a particular amount of love. To conceive of love as a need would render the beloved a mere means to personal self-fulfillment. Instead, according to Marion, I "discover" as a lover that which "defines me more intimately than everything that I possess, for what I lack inhabits me" (*EP* 108). I cannot predict the love that will call me forth by sounding the shape of my need. In contrast to Aristophanes's view of love, in Marion's view, the "me" unveiled through this discovery does not exist prior to the erotic phenomenon, not in a formal conceptual realm and not here on earth. "I am no longer first as an ego who would take the other into account after the fact," but "rise up directly as lover" (*EP* 106). I become, as lover, when "I expose myself henceforward to your point of view, different from my own, and my place is defined in relation to yours" (*EP* 106).

---

[7] Plato, *The Symposium*, trans. Christopher Gill (New York: Penguin, 2005), 26–32.

Based on Marion's description of the other as a place "out there" defining my place, I will argue in the next chapter that a work of literature can provide the emplacement essential for selfhood if not the flesh that leads to the ego's more complete emergence. Immersing ourselves a work's alter signification, readers discover what we desire; we realize what we lack. Literature does not provide what we previously knew ourselves to be lacking. This means that theories of reading based on the reader's poverty—not enough knowledge, not enough depth of emotion, not enough appreciation for beauty—are incompatible with the erotic phenomenon. For Marion it is always love's coming forth that matters, and that is something that literature can train us for. The metaphor of "training" here reinforces that reading literature gives us practice rather than an abstract object. We do not train to acquire new muscles, but instead work to strengthen the muscles we have in order to perform a particular activity better. Similarly, neither reading nor loving creates a new object: "The lover does not constitute erotic phenomenon like new objects, annexed to the mass of those that he already knows" (*EP* 216–217). Well-thumbed pages and use-loosened bindings provide evidence that reading, like loving, does not produce new objects. If reading produced an object—a new insight to be stored away for later use, or a new aesthetic modality to be pulled from an imaginary mental cupboard when needed—then one reading of a book would suffice. We would acquire the object and revisit that insight or that modality rather than revisiting the book. Instead, readers return to favorite places "out there" in fiction throughout life.

In the second step of the erotic phenomenon, the lover realizes that "Does anyone out there love me?" is in fact the wrong question. The question removes the "I" from the subject position and acknowledges it as constructed through another person, but it does not go far enough. If we wait for confirmation of another's love, then we have entered a conditional exchange, and love is unconditional. Rather than stop at wondering whether someone out there loves us, we must ask instead "Can I love first?" (*EP* 72). We must commit to loving first or we cannot love at all. Marion calls this stage in the erotic phenomenon "the radicalized erotic reduction" and designates the willingness to love first "the lover's advance" (*EP* 89, 91).

Marion focuses on the lover's advance as the moment when we begin to become ourselves. In the act of loving first, and I will argue the act of reading erotically, we do the only thing that we can "properly assume" as our own (*EP* 76).

> I do not become myself when I simply think, doubt, or imagine, because others can think my thoughts, which in any case most often do not concern me but, instead, the object of my intentionalities; nor do I become myself when I will, desire, or hope, for I never know if I do so in the first person or only as the mask which hides (and is propped up by) drives, passions, and needs that play within me, yet without me. But I become myself definitively each time and for as long as I, as lover, can love first. (*EP* 76)

The lover's advance preserves the importance of the other "out there" because it is the combination of our intentional loving and the beloved's counter-intentionality that makes and remakes us. But, Marion insists that "In order to be qualified as lover, I have only to decide to perform love's advance, a decision that depends only on me" (*EP* 91). Loving first is "the pure projection into the erotic reduction" (*EP* 91). Even if the lover cannot predetermine the way love will happen when it happens (and indeed he must not try), he can decide to love. Because this decision lies with the lover alone, a reader can decide to read in love, practicing the lover's advance and the opening of himself to a signification that comes from "out there."

This also means, however, that a reader does not have to make this decision. There are ways of reading outside of the erotic reduction. As Joshua Landy phrases it, "there is always a choice to be made; ... a text issues offers, not injunctions." Or more directly, "I must ... be good already in order to use texts" the way that influential ethical critics Martha Nussbaum and Wayne Booth recommend.[8] In the terms of the erotic reduction, I must already accept that love matters most in order to use texts to help me love loving. That is as far as reading can take us into erotic phenomena—the lover's advance. It can help us love to love. But, as I hope to show, that is quite an accomplishment. We read "hoping to love the other a little, thanks to the love of love" (*EP* 93).

When we reach the point where we ask "Can I love first?" with those whom we love in person, we realize that we are in the presence of a specific alterity capable of loving us. We relate to one another, perhaps, through the

[8] Landy, *How to Do Things*, 13 and 38–39.

gaze, perhaps through the flesh and accomplish the crossed phenomenon that rescues us from the vanity of the epistemic or ontological reductions. We answer the question "Can I love first" in the affirmative, but realize that our love's fulfillment could only be accomplished if the other has taken the same risk. We then arrive at the third step, the realization that "You loved me first" (*EP* 215). When we find that we are engaged in the erotic phenomenon, love "contaminate[s] the totality of [our] inner [lives]" (*EP* 95). It overwhelms us. As "a lived experience of consciousness," love affects "not only my emotional, but also my intellectual life, not only my conscious, but also my unconscious life" (*EP* 95). As ever imperfect lovers, we cannot rest in a single enacting of the erotic phenomenon. We are always working on love and letting someone's love work on us. Consequently, we may lose this assurance and seek it again, from the same beloved or a new one, but we remain somewhere within the erotic reduction. "To give up on asking (oneself) the question 'Does anybody love me?' Or above all to give up on the possibility of a positive response implies nothing less than giving up on the human itself" (*EP* 21).

The receptive reader

In order to understand the differences between the ways that books call us forth and the ways that people call us forth, it is necessary to return to intentionality and intuition and to add a third term signification. Since we are never just conscious, but instead are conscious *of* something, intentionality shapes our experience of the world. The world might be said to shape us in return through intuition, what it gives to us.[9] Mediating between intention and intuition is signification, which is the system of meaning-making that allows intentionality to receive intuition. Signification can be thought of as the terms through which I receive the world.[10] Our personal processes of signification

---

[9] One of Marion's major contributions to phenomenology has been his insistence on the givenness of intuition. He devotes two books to the topic: *Reduction and Givenness: Investigations of Husserl, Heidegger and Phenomenology* (orig. 1989), trans. Thomas A. Carlson (Evanston, IL.: Northwestern University Press, 1998); and *Being Given: Toward a Phenomenology of Givenness.* (orig. 1997), trans. Jeffrey L. Kosky (Stanford: Stanford University Press, 2002).

[10] Marion discusses the process of signification in *The Visible and the Revealed*, trans. Christina Gschwandtner (New York: Fordham University Press, 2008), 127–133.

bear the mark of others' language use. They enable communication through understanding, but also limit intuition by giving it shape. Robert Louis Stevenson provides a charming illustration of the concept in his novel *Treasure Island*. While searching the island for a coracle, Jim Hawkins beholds "huge slimy monsters—soft snails as it were, of incredible bigness—two or three score of them together, making the rocks to echo with their barkings."[11] Jim has never before seen sea lions. He cannot assign them a name, but more than this, he has no prior categories that succeed in helping him understand them at all—not animal, not monster, not dog, nor cephalopod.

In Marion's phenomenology, signification works differently for things we subject to understanding and for people, whom the lover always knows will confound understanding. "Thought as understanding ... owes its perfection to its refusal to be individualized" whereas people and works of literature always retain their individualization (*EP* 39).[12] Understanding "proceeds according to the universal, works upon the universilizable, and operates by universalizing" (*EP* 39). Rhododendrons, for example, can be universalized in a way that people and works of literature cannot. They may bloom under different names in different parts of the world. The category that defines a rhododendron may have different boundaries. My experience of seeing a particular rhododendron suddenly all a-blossom may be unique, and within the phenomenological reduction it is my responsibility to recognize it as such. But, the thinking about bushes blooming "proceeds according to the universal." Thought as understanding characterizes "scientific and juridical discourse" (*EP* 39). It cannot adequately characterize engagement between people. Were I to attempt, through my own resources of signification "to represent the other to me," it would "degrade the other to the dishonorable status of an object, which I could constitute at will and modify at leisure" (*EP* 98), just as I could imagine a barren hillside "modified" into bloom. Anyone attempting to impose his own signification upon another person enters into

---

[11] Robert Louis Stevenson, *Treasure Island* (Oxford: Oxford University Press, 2011), 124.

[12] Marion here departs from Husserl, who suggests in the second volume of his *Logical Investigations* that we view people via their proper names with a "double-sidedness" that allows for a simple understanding of some of a person's traits while also allowing "possibilities of further determination." Edmund Husserl, *Logical Investigations* (orig. 1901), 2 vols, trans. Dermot Moran (New York: Routledge, 2001), Vol. 2: 52.

very dubious territory because he then "cover[s] up the other and hide[s] him, or worse, destroy[s] him" (*EP* 99).

Literature, in its singularity, comes to us as neither object nor person. It has signification, presents itself to us through intuition, but cannot intend us. The beloved, in contrast, can intend me, and in the fully accomplished erotic phenomenon, the beloved gives himself to me, but on his own terms, by bursting through any signification I might have held. Reading literature, I wait, as I would for a beloved "for a new signification to thwart my own significations and impose upon me, for the first time, an alterity that transcends my advance even toward loving to love" (*EP* 98). A work of literature's singularity demands that I wait because it confounds the universalizing processes of thought that characterize scientific or juridical discourse. This is not to say that a reader could not refuse literature's demand to wait for the thwarting of her own signification and barrel on ahead, reading a work of literature as though it *were* a scientific or juridical discourse. Reading for "evidence" of a pre-conceived argument falls into this trap, as does reading for a moral. These sorts of readings degrade a work to "the dishonorable status of an object" and have no place in the erotic reduction. In fact, the habit of reading literature to reinforce a preconceived moral or to confirm a preconceived hypothesis trains us in a process of objectifying the other that is as bad for our progress as lovers as reading erotically is good. Both lovers and works of literature, then, are singular, but when we wait for the signification offered by a lover, we await a "a signification [that comes] about from the other by way of counter-intentionality" (*EP* 100). When we experience this with a book, signification is all we are given, not counter-intentionality.

One consequence of a book's lack of intentionality is that it will not alter itself in relation to us. Readers do not have a role in the creation of the book as a thing that signifies. Stanley Fish claims that we write a book as we read it.[13] Insofar as this means that a reader's intention shapes what she receives from the book, this is correct. But books have a life of their own that Fish's formulation should not overshadow. They give themselves to being brought to life by different readers in specific and unchanging ways. Books resist our influence in a way that

---

[13] Stanley Fish, "Interpreting the Variorum," *Critical Inquiry* 2 (1976): 481–482.

people may not, and this strengthens their ability to draw us into new horizons of meaning. This is why books are particularly good at revealing "the insight rooted knowledge" Husserl was searching for. But it could be made more clear how texts do this. What do readers learn about when we become aware of the interplay of our intentionality and the givenness of a text? Why would insight-rooted knowledge be more valuable to lovers than other forms of knowledge? To answer this, I need to pry the term knowledge free from its association with information. If a book helps make visible knowledge, that knowledge is not information about ourselves or information about the book or information about the world, at least not knowledge that can be stated propositionally. New Critics made this argument in their defense of poems' independence from the world that gave rise to them, but their division of literature and life presupposes that knowledge about life is primarily propositional. The knowledge that we use most in love is not. It is rather a knowing, as in a knowing look or a knowing gesture, a site of awareness that we can inhabit without needing to describe it. The insight-rooted knowledge that literature promotes enables a specific privileged relation to the world rather than conveying a collection of facts about it. It is thus knowledge we inhabit more than acquire.

Merleau-Ponty describes the knowingness of our body in a way that parallels the knowingness we find by contemplating our interaction with books:

> [W[e have found underneath the objective and detached knowledge of the body that other knowledge which we have of it in virtue of its always being with us and of the fact that we are our body. In the same way we shall need to reawaken our experience of the world as it appears to us in so far as we are in the world through our body, and in so far as we perceive the world with our body.[14]

We can similarly reawaken our experience of a text. We can become aware of our manner of encountering a poem, for example, as we might become aware of our hips while walking. Our hips function, for most of us, whether we think about them or not. An increased awareness of them during walking might render us less graceful rather than more so. But we *can* bring attention to their manner of working and acquire knowledge by doing so.

[14] Merleau-Ponty, *Phenomenology of Perception*, 239.

In a reading of Edna St. Vincent Millay's "What Lips My Lips Have Kissed and Where and Why," I can become aware of the tension between the length of the line and the length of a sentence in something like the way I bring attention to my hips.

> What lips my lips have kissed, and where, and why,
> I have forgotten, and what arms have lain
> Under my head till morning;

That first *line* can be read as though followed by an exclamation point, but by the time I get to the end of the *sentence* that inflection has to be revised. My awareness of the tension created between my first reading (prioritizing line-length) and my second reading (prioritizing syntax) can now carry me in several directions. I could attend to the relationship between syntax and line in the rest of the poem. I could ask myself why I read the first line in such a celebratory fashion to begin with. My answer could carry me into a personal past or my knowledge of Millay, or the force of the poem could detain me and make me desire nothing more than to read the next line. I can discipline my mind to follow any of these directions just like I can decide to move my hips differently, but the awareness of the potential that these lines have offered me is itself a kind of knowledge if we count knowledge as knowing or savoir faire. This awareness of the potential that a text offers (Marion would say awareness of a gift) requires cultivation. It is not a fact (poems propose their own multiple ways of being read) that one can accede to once and for all. It is a generative awareness.

Husserl calls the process of considering these possibilities "imaginative variation." In his *Cartesian Meditations*, he discusses imaginative variation using the example of a table:

> Starting from this table-perception, we vary the perceptual object, table, with a completely free optionalness, yet in such a manner that we keep perception fixed as perception of something, no matter what. Perhaps we begin by fictively changing the shape or the color of the object quite arbitrarily ... Abstaining from acceptance of its being, we change the fact of this perception into pure possibility, one among other quite "optional" pure possibilities.[15]

---

[15] Edmund Husserl, *The Essential Husserl: Basic Writings in Transcendental Phenomenology*, ed. Donn Welton (Bloomington: Indiana University Press, 1999), 310.

The purpose for doing this is not to create a new thing that substitutes for or overlays the perceptual object, but to see the object as it really is. Performing an imaginative variation, we ask: how much can my perception of this table (or poem) change and have it still be the table or poem before me? The thing being looked at is "unconditioned," which means it gives itself "prior to all concepts." Husserl values imaginative variation as a way of getting a clearer view of the essence or *eidos* of the object he beholds. In literary criticism, the practice can be valuable without assuming that a poem such as Millay's sonnet has an essence.

Imaginatively varying interpretations of a poem exposes the boundaries within which hermeneutic possibilities can proliferate. There are some interpretations that might seem reasonable at first (i.e., reading the first line of Millay's sonnet as though it had an exclamation point), but that cannot be sustained without contradicting some other element present in the poem. But more than that, imaginative variation clarifies the many interpretive options that a poem offers and invites our contemplation of how these options show themselves. I compared reading to welcoming a guest earlier. The imaginative variation appropriate for poems or novels resembles that which we might perform with a human guest more than what Husserl performs with his table. A host imagines what the guest might like for dinner based on his memory of that person, things the guest says during the present stay, and his imagination of what good things the evening could hold. Imaginative variation, with a guest as with a work of literature, does not aim to discover an essence but to facilitate an optimal experience—a dinner or a reading that reflects savoir faire. Since both literature and the welcomed guest overwhelm our plans for them, the metaphor of welcoming a work of literature serves as a reminder that imaginative variation is a practice of receiving a poem or novel, not an act of containing one. Art resembles the beloved in its ability to violently rearrange our expectations during an encounter, regardless of the number of variations we had imagined beforehand, but both the process of expanding our reception of text/guest through imaginative variation and the text/guest's overwhelming that reception move us forward in love.

In 1999, Lawrence Buell predicted that "the staying power of literary-ethical inquiry will depend" in part on its "emphasis on interhumanity" being "better synthesized with a social and/or political ethics."[16] Marion's erotic phenomenon allows for this synthesis and can account for literature's role in it. Marion himself shies away from discussing the social and ethical implications of his philosophy, perhaps because one cannot truly receive the gift of saturated phenomenon with a concept of what that phenomenon will lead to already in mind.[17] Other people confront us as mysterious in their unknowability but also mysteriously precious as a figures in the evolving interhumanity of which we too are a part. If we were to turn to another person with an ethical precept already in mind, then the conceptual structure of our intuition would threaten to block out our vision of him or her. Even the most admirable social principles can, according to this logic, threaten to obliterate the gift that the other person is and replace that gift, that liveliness, with a politicized object. Feeding the hungry seems like an indisputably good political goal. However, if we encounter another person as a mouth to be fed—an opportunity for charitable action and potentially for self-gratification—we lose the gift of being overwhelmed by that person's individual humanity, a humanity that prompts us to share food in the recognition of shared need.

Marion alludes to the danger of this sort of objectification in both *The Erotic Phenomenon* and *The Reason of the Gift*. However, neither Marion's silence about the social implications of his work, nor the danger of objectification indicates that the erotic phenomenon does not have implications for social ethics. The caution against viewing others in light of our social, ethical, or political goals is itself an ethical gesture in the common use of the term *ethics*. Marion exhorts us to ask ourselves what we can do for another's good because this is love's command, but the answer to this question arises from within the uniqueness of who we are, who the other is and who each of us is becoming through the other.[18] The social ethic that arises from Marion's explanation of our "interhumanity" is not that of the regional or the sociological category, but that of the neighbor, the family, the lover, and beloved, which we must recognize ourselves to be from our first encounter with each individual other.

---

[16] Lawrence Buell, "Introduction: In Pursuit of Ethics," *PMLA* 114, no.1 (January 1999): 16.
[17] For Marion's thoughts on the end of ethics, see his "The Freedom to be Free" in *Prolegomena to Charity*, trans. Thomas A. Carlson (Evanston, IL: Northwestern University Press, 1998), 31–52.
[18] Jean-Luc Marion, *In the Self's Place*, trans. Jeffrey L. Kosky (Palo Alto: Stanford University Press, 2012), 279.

The warning against trapping people in our own conception of them (political, social, ethical, or otherwise) has implications for the way we read as well. In order to give a book room to operate on us as an intuition and signification that comes to us from elsewhere, we must try to refrain from imposing concepts on it prior to reading. The erotic phenomenon proceeds through a reader's or a lover's willingness to cede control without ceding attention to the text or the beloved other giving itself. Although the erotic phenomenon begins with a subject asking "Does anybody out there love me?" which a text, intentionless as it is, cannot answer, it soon becomes clear that the question that actually allows love to operate is "Can I love first?" Can I allow myself to be altered by an intentionality and signification that arises from elsewhere? Literary texts offer signification autonomous enough to both invite and resist my intentionality. As long as I allow my intentionality to be overcome by what the text gives, then the process of learning how to let the text come forth can renew the insight-rooted knowledge that Husserl privileges. That insight-rooted knowledge does not collapse back into the cognitive reduction, but instead makes me aware of the possibilities that a work of art or another person uniquely enables. By imaginatively varying the intentionality I direct toward a text, I recognize the scope of possible reading events that a text can give rise to as well as the ways an alternative signification can resist the signification I expect and posit its own.

3

The Lover's Advance

Is the phenomenon of reading similar enough to the phenomenon of love for one to instruct the other? Put another way, can books induce the "radical alterity of the ego to itself" that the erotic reduction requires (*EP* 25)? Although he concerns himself mostly with the beloved in the flesh, Marion himself alludes to the possibility of nonpersons providing this alterity. Landscapes and cities, he suggests, "can deploy good or ill against me." The crucial requirement seems to be that I am "susceptible to a decision, which does not belong to me and which determines me in advance, because it comes to me from elsewhere" (*EP* 25).

Certainly books impose decisions upon us. Readers of Sherlock Holmes's adventures famously did not want the sleuth to die, protesting the possibility of his death to his creator Arthur Conan Doyle.[1] But over the waterfall he went, locked in battle with Professor Moriarty. Doyle brings Holmes back in *The Hound of the Baskervilles* and "The Adventure of the Empty House," but the desire of thousands of English readers was not enough to stop that fall. The decision was out of their control. My students' fury at Shakespeare flares every semester that I teach *Romeo and Juliet*. "Why," they demand to know, "could Romeo not have waited a few more minutes before drinking poison?" But, Romeo drains the vial, as he has drained it for over four hundred years. A reader can make decisions about a book. During or after the event of reading, she may reflect on Romeo's death as both an element of the text's structure and

---

[1] Janet Pascal, *Arthur Conan Doyle: Beyond Baker Street* (Oxford: Oxford University Press, 2000), 76–78.

an event that affects her emotionally. But, the story of his death imposes itself as a "radical alterity" that she cannot on a first reading anticipate, and can never control.

In his "Phenomenology of Reading," George Poulet explains that when we read, we open the door and invite a book to dwell in us in much the same way that Marion describes us inviting in the beloved. The book, Poulet says, ceases to be an object and becomes "a series of words, of images, of ideas which in their turn begin to exist ... in my inner most self."[2] Books, viewed as potential phenomena, have their origin in us; they "begin to exist" in us. We also expand our existence through them as they become part of our "inner most" selves, selves that, under the erotic reduction, only come into being through our participation in love. Books intercede in the erotic phenomenon at the point where we ask "Can I love first?" They provide an "alterity of the other" that is "unsubstitutable" and that "affects me from out there, beginning from itself" (*EP* 98), which Marion says can admit me to the erotic reduction.

This "alterity of the other" cannot be an object because an object, as discussed in the last chapter, would be something that "I could constitute at will and modify at my leisure" (*EP* 98). But books, as we see with Romeo's and Sherlock's deaths, resist modification by their readers after a point. In reading, as in loving, I must "wait for ... the unpredictable arrival of a signification, coming to contradict my intention *with its own*" (*EP* 98). In both cases, the signification that comes to me will be "unpredictable" and "unsubstitutable" and will begin "from itself." It is a book's thing-ness, its inertness, that stops the erotic reduction from moving forward beyond the lover's advance when we read. "[T]he things of this world," as Marion writes, "quite simply do not affect me such as they are, nor do they make me feel anything about them in themselves—for the simple and radical reason that they do not feel themselves or experience anything as their action" (*EP* 113). We can ask, "Can I love first?" We can answer ourselves in the affirmative and open ourselves to the creation of a phenomenon of reading. We can embrace, in this phenomenon, the suspension of our intuition about a book and can enjoy the process of being changed if we allow the signification of a

---

[2] Poulet, "Phenomenology of Reading," 54.

book, coming from outside our egological sphere, to work on us. But, unlike a person, a book does not receive the intuition I offer it. It does not intend me. The erotic phenomenon, therefore, halts before achieving its completion in the realization "You loved me first." Books, of course, cannot do that. Nevertheless, the alterity of books imitates the alterity of the beloved just enough that we can practice that act of opening the door. The difference between our own pre-reading existence and the event that we add to existence by reading a book allows us to take that initializing gesture of love, to train ourselves in the act of loving first.

Loving first is the primary requirement for us as lovers and thus according to the erotic reduction, the question upon which our individual personhood depends. Marion argues that for love to escape the trap of reciprocity (*EP* 69, 72), we must be able to commit ourselves to loving with no promise of return. "[I]n order to be qualified as a lover," he explains,

> I have only to decide to perform love's advance, a decision that depends only on me, even though it always plays out at the limits of my abilities. To decide to love does not assure loving, but it does assure deciding to love. And the lover attests himself lover precisely through this decision—the first and the purest, without a cause, without return, a pure projection in to the erotic reduction, without any other reason than itself. (*EP* 91)

The reader's decision to perform the lover's advance varies with each book. The lover's advance may be described as the moment when a lover or reader engages in creating an event that becomes part of the lover or reader's emerging personhood. As a reader, I might decide to initiate the lover's advance before I begin reading. An inherited book, for example, or a book recommended by a favorite teacher may bring with it an aura of expectation that predisposes us to love. Or, the lover's advance may happen more gradually, as a book begins to shape our view of events that happen outside of its pages.

Double vision

Alain Badiou, one of Europe's foremost philosophers of love, clarifies what happens when we make the lover's advance as readers or lovers-in-person.

Badiou has addressed love in detail in *In Praise of Love* (2012) and *Conditions* (2008). In *Conditions*, he writes that "love does not involve prostrating the Same before the alter of the Other.... [L]ove is not even an experience of the other, but an experience of the world, of the situation under the post-evental condition that there are Two."[3] Badiou here stresses the cooperative nature of love, that it does not stabilize categories of difference—Same, Other—but instead creates a new way of viewing the world that could only come into being through the unique process of one lover's imagining another's experience. After all, when lovers speak to each other, they are often not speaking about themselves as lovers. They speak as lovers about the world that includes them. Reading offers the two-ness Badiou describes. During a reading, the images gaining form and words gaining voice in a reader's "inner most self" are a composite of the text's signification and the reader's imaginative construction based on past experience. Together text and reader create an event, and that event of reading, like other events where we admit a "radical alterity" has the potential to affect the people that we are continually becoming.

Writing *In Praise of Love*, Badiou says, "Love is always the possibility of being present at the birth of a world."[4] One lover's awareness of the other lover's vision creates a new way of looking, a new world of event-mental experience. Books, too, create this double vision. The lover knows, however, that the beloved retains his independence. In the moment of shared looking, each lover depends on the other, but neither one subjects himself to the other. Rather, both subject themselves to the vision, and the event of love being created. Books, being stable, cannot allow for the "constant re-birth of the world" that Badiou says is the privilege of a long relationship with the beloved.[5] But, they do facilitate double vision for as long as we read them and the experience of two-ness they offer becomes a permanent part of us. Reading them again and again throughout our lives, works of literature facilitate a "re-birth of the world" multiple times. Books also exhibit the independence of a lover. As with Sherlock's and Romeo's un-wished-for deaths, they are guaranteed to resist change after a point, whereas the changes that two long-time lovers undergo

---

[3] Alain Badiou, *Conditions*, trans. Steve Corcoran (London: Continuum, 2008), 182.
[4] Alain Badiou, *In Praise of Love*, trans. Peter Bush (New York: The New Press, 2012), 26.
[5] Badiou, *In Praise*, 41.

are always fluid. Books thus give us extra practice in modifying our own vision without the expectation of a reciprocal change in the other's engaged vision.

Reading Wordsworth's "Lines Written a Few Miles Above Tintern Abbey," for example, I imagine seeing "plots of cottage-ground" and "hedge-rows" that are "hardly hedge-rows," but instead "little lines/ Of sportive wood run wild" (lines 11, 16–17). The hedgerows in my vision of the poem look like Yorkshire hedgerows because that is what I have seen, whereas the Tintern Abbey hedge-rows are Welsh. Nevertheless, the hedge-rows that Wordsworth and I make together need both his Welsh and my Yorkshire vision. In the presence of my beloved, we could adjust to one another, pointing out elements of the scene below us that the other might have missed, but in the presence of a poem, I, the reader, have to do all the adjusting. The description of the hedgerows and surrounding countryside in the poem reads as follows:

> Five years have past; five summers, with the length
> Of five long winters! and again I hear
> These waters, rolling from their mountain-springs
> With a sweet inland murmur.—Once again
> Do I behold these steep and lofty cliffs,
> Which on a wild secluded scene impress
> Thoughts of more deep seclusion; and connect
> The landscape with the quiet of the sky.
> The day is come when I again repose
> Here, under this dark sycamore, and view
> These plots of cottage-ground, these orchard-tufts,
> Which, at this season, with their unripe fruits,
> Among the woods and copses lose themselves,
> Nor, with their green and simple hue, disturb
> The wild green landscape. Once again I see
> These hedge-rows, hardly hedge-rows, little lines
> Of sportive wood run wild; (lines 1–17)[6]

According to the altered vision the poem offers me, the cottage-ground must not be imagined as static, but must be seen as having changed over a

---

[6] William Wordsworth, "Lines Written a Few Miles Above Tintern Abbey," *The Major Works*, ed. Stephen Gill (Oxford: Oxford University Press, 2008), 131–135.

five-year period. My vision of the scene must attend to a wildness that the cottage plots cannot counteract, and that infects the wood. But the poem's series of demonstrative pronouns reminds me that no matter how much I adjust my picture of these cottage grounds and hedgerows, I can never actually access the vision signified by the poem. I can never see "*These* plots of cottage-ground" at "*this* season" with "*their* unripe fruits." Because I intend this scene in my imagination rather than in person, I am free to continue adjusting my vision to meet Wordsworth's, but the reading experience reminds me that I can never free myself of the condition of my separateness from the embodied experience signified by the poem. Literary works provide practice in decentering our own perspective and experiencing the world from "the point of view of difference, point by point," which Badiou says characterizes our experience of love.[7] The fact that literature alludes through its formal constructedness to the fact that it cannot offer the time- and place-bound experience of "these" hedgerows also reminds readers of the continued autonomy of another's vision.

Because works of literature add to rather than represent the world, literary hedgerows admit a degree of malleability that actual trees and bushes resist. Dr. Seuss, for example, makes his truffula trees smell like "butterfly milk," a scent that overthrows quite violently the intuition most adults have of trees. A poem about a hedgerow can allow for a more radical displacement of our own intuition than the often common-law phenomenon of viewing an actual hedgerow beside my lover. The change between my pre-evental singular vision, and my post-evental (in this case post-reading) vision, where I am aware of having been changed by a vision radically different from my own, is potentially greater. Those literary works that overwhelm and alter our intuition the most offer us a particular sort of practice in the lover's advance. They help us practice opening ourselves to radical alterity that will demand great changes in our perspective regardless of how much we resist that demand.

A poem entitled "Hedgerows" by Stanley Plumly demands that our vision of hedgerows change more radically than the hedgerow description in "Tintern Abbey."

---

[7] Badiou, *In Praise*, 56.

I think, for a moment, I wanted to die,
and that somehow the tangle
and bramble, the branch and flowering of the hedge
would take me in, torn, rendered down
to the apple or the red wound or the balm,
the green man, leaf and shred.
I think I wanted the richness, the thickness,
the whole dumb life gone to seed,
and the work to follow, the hedger with his tools,
tethering and cutting, wood and mind. (lines 30–39)[8]

Here Plumly's speaker longs for another power, "the hedger with his tools," to come impose order on his life, but his longing is so entangled with the image of the hedge that we cannot extract it. We could subject the poem to a simple symbolic reading. We could imagine that the apple stands for his life's fruit—maybe his poetry—and that this opposes his "dumb life" —maybe his inexpressible life that "goes to seed" and produces things he cannot control. We can suggest that "the red wound" stands in for the possibility of his life being rendered down to something other than the fruit it has produced—maybe the pain he has brought into the world. Our vision of the poem could resist further alteration. We could stubbornly and symbolically picture books of poems between the branches of a regular hedg-y looking hedge. Or, we could react to the poem by refusing to make the lover's advance at all, by refusing to change our vision of hedges even enough to try to make sense of Plumly's verse. A reader could recognize that the vision expressed in this poem is so radically different from his usual intuition of hedges that he refuses to engage with such radical alterity. But that would be a loss. An event lies implicit in this poem, waiting for a reader who can accommodate the unique double vision that the poem and reader could create together. But, in order to create that double vision, the reader must allow the poem to decide some things for him.

If, contrary to these resistant modes of reading, I begin reading a poem called "Hedgerows" determined to make with it whatever vision we can accomplish together, with an intuition, as Marion puts it, "that is at once

8 Stanley Plumly, "Hedgerows," *The Atlantic Monthly* 259, no. 6 (June 1987): 46–47.

intentional toward the other and without an assignable other" (*EP* 96), then having made the (book) lover's advance, I can make a significant event of my reading. Significant, first, in that my reading can become an event that has a chance to help create me, and second, in that I will have one more experience in which I admitted a signification arising from outside myself. Reading like a lover, I see that the poem's "I" wanted "richness" and "thickness" and that isolating "apple" as poetic fruit and "red wound" as pain he has created denies this richness and thickness. The apple and wound, the balm, which suggests the healing of the wound, cannot be "rendered down" as separable parts of the hedge without doing the living hedge significant damage. The narrator can separate them with an "or" in his linguistic statement about the hedge, but the image of the hedge invoked through the statement reunites them. The poem's images of "tangle and bramble," "flowering," "richness," and "thickness" belie not a desire to have one's life separated into the production of pleasant fruit and painful wound, but a desire to remain as complex as the living hedge. The syntax itself, strung together over six lines in the first sentence, with eight phrases ranging chaotically from one word—"torn"—to eleven words—"the branch and flowering of the hedge would take me in"—also suggests a desire to resist simplification. The balanced syntax of the last line—"tethering and cutting, wood and mind"—with its two tidy parallel pairs implies that the hedger with his tools can hope to curb the living complexity of the hedge for a season. But, only living hedges need hedgers with tools. The "I" who apparently no longer wants to die but for a moment did, wants to retain "richness," fruit and flower, whether he is dead or not.

In the poem's last lines a boy comes and sits by the hedge

> having come from the field
> with his family, half hungry, half cold,
> one more day of the harvest accounted,
> yellowing, winnowing,
> the boy lost in the thought
> of the turning of the year and the dead father. (lines 45–50)

And there at the end is our hedger. A child, perhaps the dead speaker's child, offers the only hope the poetic speaker has of obtaining both death, which offers to stabilize his life in a way that someone can at least for a season make sense of it, and life, in the continuance of fruit and wound and flower and balm. Reading like a lover, I can see much more than a hedge here. The strangeness and irreducible singularity of the poem's vision decides for me that this will turn into a poem exploring legacies and aging and what lasts and goes to seed after we fall dumb. The poem also requires a kind of vision that cannot be reduced to an image, symbol, or message. It has to be lived through as an event.

I do not mean to imply that reading Stanley Plumly's "Hedgerows" somehow makes us better lovers than reading Wordsworth's "Tintern Abbey." First, and most simply, this cannot be the case because the entirety of Wordsworth's poem, which I have not quoted here, makes difficult demands on a reader's vision that I have not discussed. Second, and more importantly, the poems themselves remain inert things. There are a lot of variables that affect the kind of phenomenon that a reading of a poem will become, and therefore there are a lot of variables that affect the extent to which a reading can offer us practice as lovers. The vision of a poem might differ so radically from ours that we cannot adjust enough to let it change us. Or we may not make the effort. A reader's acts of love will be as unique as his acts of love in person. The practice, however, of waiting for the signification of an other and building a vision of the world in cooperation with that signification will be equally valuable for every love.

Some loves

Although I think that Marion has articulated new philosophical grounds for reading in love, the phenomenon of reading in love is not new. The great nineteenth-century English critic William Hazlitt writes like a lover when he says of Shakespeare's *Cymbeline* that "the reading of this play is like going [on] a journey with some uncertain object at the end of it."[9] He implies the "twoness" of vision that Badiou characterized as love's view of the world by suggesting that he and the play would see new things on their journey together. When, in 1909, György Lukács speaks in the voice of an impassioned reader

---

[9] William Hazlitt, *Characters of Shakespeare's Plays* (London: John Templeton, 1838), 1.

in "Richness, Chaos, and Form: A Dialogue Concerning Laurence Sterne," he writes: "The reason why [Sterne's works] really matter to us is, after all, that they show us a way into life, a new way toward the enrichment of our life." He describes the "overwhelmingly powerful effect of Sterne's writing," calling it "richness as an ethic, knowing how to live, knowing how to draw life from everything that comes to hand."[10] Here Lukács adopts the metaphor of seeing double, saying that literature "shows us a way" and exposes "richness." He also points out that the change in vision continues to affect us after the journey of a particular book has finished. Mohsin Hamid, a contemporary novelist, chooses a more corporeal metaphor:

> And in reading about a seafarer, you found yourself intimate with another human being in a way that was unlike your other intimacies, for even those you loved most, you loved from the outside, but with the characters in books you moved inside, and the boundaries between you and them began to shimmer and dissolve. This experience was both new and familiar to you. All human beings come into existence inside another human being, a human being we call our mother, but we cannot recall that time afterwards, and so reading a book, entering inside another human consciousness, is both a revelation and a return to our source.[11]

Hamid here reverses the language of most reader-oriented critics. Rather than describing how the reader gives life to the books, he has the book give life to the reader.

Alberto Manguel is a shameless and profligate lover of books, exhibiting his affairs in seven separate works, some complete with pictures. In *A Reader on Reading*, he describes "the craft of reading" and explains that "beyond the author's intentions and the reader's hopes, a book can make us better and wiser." As a boy, he traveled so much that books provided a "story-land homecoming" in the absence of an actual home. Books "seduce" him, he writes.[12] He does not hesitate to compare reading to the physical and spiritual extremes of love. "Reading or making love," he writes, "we should be able to

---

[10] György Lukács, "Richness, Chaos, and Form: A Dialogue Concerning Laurence Sterne," *Soul and Form*, ed. John T. Sanders and Katie Terezakis (New York: Columbia University Press, 2010), 169.

[11] Mohsin Hamid, "Living in the Age of Permawar," *The Guardian*, 22 August 2015.

[12] Alberto Manguel, *A Reader on Reading* (New Haven: Yale University Press, 2010), x, 12, and 14.

lose ourselves in the other, into whom—to borrow St. John's image—we are transformed: reader into writer into reader, lover into lover into lover."[13] The diverse language used by these readers to describe their loves reinforces the singularity of our experiences with books, but each of these readers illustrates individuals answering a book's invitation to create the kind of double vision we create with others in love. Another contemporary reader-in-love, Joshua Landy, has developed a useful term for the fictions he has loved. He calls them "formative fictions."[14] As different as the readers quoted above are, they share this sense of reading as formative, and they express literature's ability to form us in intersubjective terms. They operate from a tacit agreement that books change us in much the same way as people change us.

The most well-known spokesperson for love and reading is Martha Nussbaum, whose essays in *Love's Knowledge* articulate literature's position in an Aristotelian pursuit of ethics. Nussbaum's work has inspired several valuable reexaminations of literary theory and ethics by fans and naysayers and has provided an important, if sometimes unacknowledged, basis for new cognitive examinations of the ethics of reading. The practice of reading that she exemplifies has much in common with the practice of reading I think the erotic reduction inspires. However, the phenomenological view of a book as a potential for activity differs from a cognitive approach that treats books as objects whose only action can be to represent a world that exists outside the books' covers. For cognitivists, the world outside the book is where the potential for ethical activity exists. For phenomenologists, the event of reading takes its place beside other events. Consequently, a phenomenological view of reading allows for the possibility that books can change us by adding to our experience rather than merely representing possible experiences to us. I should stress that reading erotically does gain its importance from our post-reading engagement with nonfictional embodied people. I share Nussbaum's interest in "what it is for a human being to live well."[15] Happily, phenomenology allows the event of reading to itself be part of a life well lived and not just a prelude to it.

---

[13] Manguel, *A Reader on Reading*, 181.
[14] Landy, *How to Do Things*, 3 and 12.
[15] Martha Nussbaum, *Love's Knowledge: Essays on Philosophy and Literature* (Oxford: Oxford University Press, 1990), 173.

Nussbaum wants readers to think of themselves as whole people. She argues that in order to be morally responsible agents we need to train our affections as well as our understanding. In particular, she contends that "practical reason unaccompanied by emotion is not sufficient for practical wisdom" because emotional habits developed through a life of ethical discernment are more likely to determine our actions than abstract universal rules.[16] Novels merit a place in a life well-lived because they "direct us to the concrete; they display before us a wealth of richly realized detail, presented as relevant for choice."[17] Emotions, for Nussbaum, are an important element in our ethical training because they help us to know ourselves, to know others, and to know what to do to live well. Love receives pride of place among other emotions by being featured in the title of her essay collection on philosophy and literature and by inspiring some of her most moving rhetoric. But, for her, love derives its value from epistemology. Love itself is not Nussbaum's goal. *Love's Knowledge* is. Whether we do anything with that knowledge is another question. In Landy's recent critique of Nussbaum, he points out that according to Nussbaum's view of love as a motivating emotion for ethics (rather than a foundational condition as I am suggesting), "there is nothing whatsoever to prevent us from taking an intensive, vigorous, sustained, detailed, painstaking interest in the entanglements of other lives while remaining entirely remote from the moral fray."[18]

Furthermore, Nussbaum's language of "ethical engagement" and "agency" presumes a metaphysical separation between a self and the world that cannot be sustained under the erotic reduction. In Marion's terms, I do not have an independent self with a history of moral agency that makes a decision to love someone else because I see a rational reason for doing so. Rather, I am already involved in love. If I am old enough and educated enough to be reading novels, love has already had its hand on me. I do not decide to rise from my reading couch and seek out someone who needs my love, or who needs my ethical behavior in any way. I recognize that loving, being loved, and longing for love constitutes me through my relationships to others, already.

---

[16] Nussbaum, *Love's Knowledge*, 40.
[17] Nussbaum, *Love's Knowledge*, 95.
[18] Landy, *How to Do Things*, 34.

In conclusion, making the lover's advance one time is enough to locate us within the boundaries of the erotic reduction, but what poor lovers we would be with no more practice than this. In order for the practice that reading gives us to matter, it must be repeated. After repeatedly awaiting signification from elsewhere and repeatedly creating new visions of the world that accommodate the vision of a literary work, waiting and creating with our embodied, nonliterary loves might get easier. Reading in love, expanding our capacity for love through reading, does not happen with one book, but a lifetime of reading. Ultimately our selves depend on others for the articulation of desire (*EP* 195), so the erotic reduction includes motivation to move beyond our book and love in the world, but reading gets us started. Reading helps us decide to love because it trains us in love's habits. Because the boundary between loving someone and loving to love "remains imprecise" (*EP* 92), "a border zone" (*EP* 93), these habits help us become at least sojourners in love's country. It will remain for our beloved to confirm or deny our citizenship there.

Interlude

Every reader "transforms" a book "into event and return."[1] The givenness of a text dissolves if I treat it as an "object already constituted."[2] The second part of this book involves an application of sorts, but this does not mean to apply a method of reading to various texts as though the texts were evidence by which to prove a theoretical argument. To pursue such a goal would be imply a superiority of abstract concept over the diversity of gifts that literature itself can offer. Having searched out the border of where reading can take us within the erotic reduction, I will describe in the next three chapters the experience of reading that the reduction offers. Since my own acts of reading occur as singular events, constituted between one reader and one text, the description of them makes no claim to predict another reader's experience with the same text. Instead in describing the relationships that underlie acts of reading and acts of love, I identify modes of relating to works of art and other people that will manifest themselves in every act of reading performed by someone within the erotic reduction.

The three modes of relating explored in the following chapters are empathy, attention, and being overwhelmed. I argue that by habituating us to these modes of relating to saturated phenomena generally, reading empathetically, with attention, and with a willingness to be overwhelmed can shake readers out of the habit of regarding ourselves as autonomous selves. It is all very well that Lévinas and Marion, as well as Jean-Luc Nancy, Judith Butler, Giorgio

---

[1] Jean-Luc Marion, *Givenness and Hermeneutics*, trans. Jean-Pierre Lafouge (Milwaukee, WI: Marquette University Press, 2013), 61.
[2] Marion, *Givenness and Hermeneutics*, 25.

Agamben, Derrida, and others have, from differing perspectives, besieged the walls of the autonomous self.[3] Nancy was already searching for who comes after the subject in 1986. But the act of reading philosophy does not encourage the kinds of intentionality that would make the fluid, interdependent self a regular part of conscious experience. Philosophy may encourage its readers to think with a philosopher, which is an element of empathetic relationality, but it also encourages distanced self-reflection. Do I agree with this argument being offered, the reader is invited to ask. The philosopher's own anticipation of counterarguments, his thesis and his evidential proofs, his questions and his answers all remind readers to step back and consider to what extent we want to think along with him or whether perhaps we want to think in opposition.

Even a charitable reading of philosophy, which imagines the philosopher's argument in its most convincing form, still falls short of the empathy that happens quite easily with novels. *Fugitive Pieces* by Anne Michaels, which I will discuss in Chapter 4, invites readers to imagine being sunk in mud in Poland, ranging over sun-blanched hillsides in Greece, and looking at an old man in a Toronto backyard, a most unlikely combination of events although within a realistic frame. And we do imagine. Something about the voice or voices of literary works lowers the defenses that philosophy rhetorically reinforces. Unlike the philosophical works that explain the priority of an interdependent self, this work of literature prompts readers to see how blurred the division is between themselves and the characters portrayed. It never suggests through its form that we should not open ourselves to the experiences of identification that it offers.

---

[3] See, e.g., Emmanuel Lévinas, *Totality and Infinity: Essays on Exteriority*, trans. Alphonso Lingis (Dordrecht: Kluwer Academic Press, 1991); and Judith Butler, *Senses of the Subject* (New York: Fordham University Press, 2015). Derrida's conception of selfhood is a vexed issue. He uses the language of acting much more than the language of being, but Catherine Malabou and Adrian Johnston seem to have it right when they say that "Derrida's thought may be regarded, as a whole, as a long and continuous deconstruction of auto-affection in the name of heteroaffection" where heteroaffectivity includes both the sense that "what affects me is always something other than myself" and that the acting and receiving selves within me already imply a heterogeneous experience of selfhood. *Self and Emotional Life: Philosophy, Psychoanalysis and Neuroscience*, (New York: Columbia University Press, 2013), 19–20; Jacques Derrida, *On Touching: Jean-Luc Nancy*, trans. Christine Irizarry (Stanford: Stanford University Press, 2005); Giorgio Agamben, "What is an Apparatus?" in *What is an Apparatus? and Other Essays*, trans. David Kishik and Stefan Pedatella (Stanford: Stanford University Press, 2009), 1–24, especially 14–15. An excellent recent overview of the French philosophers contesting the subject over the last two and a half decades is Irving Goh, *The Reject: Community, Politics and Religion After the Subject* (New York: Fordham University Press, 2015), especially "Let's Drop the Subject," 1–23.

Not all forms of literature invite empathy equally, but research from neuroscience, psychology, philosophy, and literary criticism has consistently indicated that literature, particularly narrative literature, leads readers through experiences of empathy that become a permanent part of them. Suzanne Keen summarizes her finding from these various fields in *Empathy and the Novel* and concludes that:

> readers' perception of a text's fictionality plays a role in subsequent empathetic response, by releasing readers from the obligations of self-protection through skepticism and suspicion. Thus they may respond with greater empathy to an unreal situation and characters because of the protective fictionality, but ... still internalize the experience of empathy in a way that promises later real-world responsiveness to others' needs.[4]

Within a phenomenological reduction that sees perceptual life as constituting the self without clearly delineated boundaries between "internal" experiences and "real-world responsiveness," the reader's amplified experience of empathy counts significantly among those acts of love that permanently change the self. Empathetic reading cannot predict empathetic action, but the act of empathetic reading signifies readers' phenomenalization of a human experience from elsewhere unencumbered by an anticipation of return, an action that accrues to the acts of love in which I recognize myself.

With attention, too, literature invites a different kind of engagement than philosophy. Richard Lanham has described the new "economics of attention" wherein attention has become the most coveted resource in labor and consumer economics. In this new attention economy the act of reading either philosophy or literature must compete with video games, social media, soccer games, and work—often many hours of work—for reader's attention. (In 2013, the Organization for Economic Co-operation and Development found that the average number of paid vacation days workers received in the US was a depressing zero.[5]) Amid this widespread cultural attention deficit, books of phenomenology and bildungsroman sit dusty on the shelves.

---

[4] Keen, *Empathy and the Novel*, xiv.
[5] Rebecca Ray, Milla Sanes, and John Schmitt, "No Vacation Nation Revisited," *Center for Economic and Policy Research* (May 2013), 2.

One thing that makes literature worth paying attention to at all is the kind of attention it invites, which is engrossed, self-forgetting intention. Professional literary scholars have sometimes scoffed at immersive reading as undertheorized and unreflective, and there is a point to be made there. The acts of reading that most enlighten other readers when recounted are never merely immersive. However, literature's invitation to immerse ourselves in the dynamic alterity of a literary text is one of its most valuable qualities within the erotic reduction. Reading literature frees us, in Marion's words, from our amorous "autism" because it can draw our attention so fully (*EP* 24).

Literature's ability to transport readers offers both promise and danger. Books may invite us to participate in characters' epiphanies, their hard-learned lessons, and creative synthesis. But, what if they invite us to participate in their racial bias, their cruelty, their indifference to the inconvenient other. There is a danger of accepting that invitation because we are attending so fully to the book's own view and not to the objections our own pre-reading view might have offered. The sense of danger that has followed novel reading in particular (oppositions to poetry, drama, autobiography, and satire are less common) since its rise in popularity in the eighteenth century makes it clear that the powerful form of attention literature invites is remarkable for its capacity to make us forget ourselves—for better or for worse.

Forgetting oneself has been constructed as both virtue and vice depending on what it is contrasted with. In the nineteenth century, working-class readers and female readers of all classes were critiqued for letting themselves be carried away by fiction because it was seen to compete with more virtuous demands on their attention—child care, domestic chores, work outside the home, or "serious" (utilitarian) reading, depending on the class and gender of the accused reader. In the twenty-first century, fiction reading is no longer viewed as a threat to these more "useful" activities, but is associated with other other-directed leisure pursuits such as volunteer work or attendance at community concerts. In the 2002 "Reading at Risk" study performed by the US Census Bureau, fewer than half of Americans surveyed had read a single book of fiction that year. This fact was much lamented. Dana Gioia, a poet and the chairman of the National Endowment of the Arts, linked reading to "active attention" and worried that the loss of "engaged literacy" would mean the loss of important "intellectual capabilities," and "the many sorts of human continuity such skills allow."[6] The once-maligned activity of immersive reading has become part of a nostalgic longing for a time when leisure was less forcibly interrupted by electronic alerts for our attention. Other forms of immersive attention that compete with reading today do not offer the same level of self-forgetfulness. Quite often, instead, they justify hours of focus on the self—pictures of one's self and one's social world in social media, or record numbers one has gained in video games, or the familiar if tiresome to-do listing of the overworked. Consequently, the once-vicious activity of reading now looks virtuous. Philosophy, important as it is, has never been accused of distracting us, the masses, from the obligations of daily life because for most people it does not invite immersive, self-forgetting attention.

A third mode of relating to literature that benefits readers' capacity to love other people is the mode of being overwhelmed. Marion describes four kinds of phenomena that he identifies as saturated: the event, the idol, the icon, and the flesh. As Chapter 6 discusses, literature saturates our intentionality in the form of the event and the idol, and it can be approached as icon. Love, too, joins the ranks of saturated phenomenality. We always experience the other as a saturated phenomenon if we really experience the other at all, through the figure of the face, which Marion describes as an icon. Love overwhelms us in a particular way in that it always, even at its most devastating, expands and benefits, even blesses the self. Literature uniquely prepares us to be overwhelmed by love because like the human other, a book as other opens itself to us more fully in relation to the intention we direct to it. As readers read, our capacity to intend a particular book is expanded, and that process looks like love.

Philosophy also gives us more as we open ourselves to it, but the "more" it gives is more knowledge, more skill performing certain kinds of thoughts, more awareness. Philosophy trades in understanding, which is shared and transferable in public because it is non-individuated. It is confined by its need to communicate identically to multiple people. Literature resembles the engagement with another person more because it offers more possibilities

---

[6] Dana Gioia, "Preface," *Reading at Risk: A Survey of Literary Reading in America: Executive Summary* (Washington, DC: National Endowment for the Arts, 2002).

of imaginative variation, more of an "endless hermeneutic." It reveals itself uniquely to each reader every time. It has the specific, unique locatedness that beloved others have so that we can return to books and people and be amazed anew.

Marion, himself a great reader of literature, signals at the beginning of *The Erotic Phenomenon* the ways in which literature can enact processes of love that philosophy can only describe. Poetry, he writes, can "liberate me from my erotic aphasia," and novels succeed "in breaking the autism of my amorous crises because it reinscribes them in a sociable, plural, and public narrativity" (*EP* 1). In Marion's metaphor, none of us are able lovers, but literature enables us in a way that philosophy itself cannot. Marion finds the strength to celebrate love and the discernment to begin describing it as a concept, but conceptualization, the honorable act of philosophy, is not the act we need most in love.

4

Empathy

Empathy has received attention lately within a variety of fields. Literary criticism, magpie discipline that it often is, has borrowed insights from neuroscience, philosophy, psychology, and sociology and used them to elaborate theories of narrative empathy and to illuminate individual literary texts.[1] Although quite diverse, the inquiries into empathy by literary critics have generally taken one of two directions. A great deal of work has been done on the neuroscience of reading literature and its implications for empathy, and a great deal of work has been done in empathy that transcends cultural difference. I begin this chapter by providing a brief overview of these two approaches to empathy and reading. Then, I describe what a phenomenological account of empathy can contribute to this growing area of literary critical practice. Finally, I narrow my focus to empathy within the erotic reduction and consider how this highly individualized and immediate conception of empathy enables new ways of describing the relationship between empathic reading and empathic practice with people in real life. As mentioned, the ease with which readers are moved to empathy makes reading both alluring and dangerous for readers committed to love. In addition to examining the manipulation of empathy in *Fugitive Pieces*, a novel that guides readers through and thematizes several different kinds of empathic encounters, I look at texts that frustrate or defy reader's

---

[1] For example, see, on the Theory of Mind, Lisa Zunshine, *Why We Read Fiction: Theory of Mind and the Novel* (Columbus: Ohio State University Press, 2006); Amy Coplan, "Empathic Engagement with Narrative Fictions," *The Journal of Aesthetics and Art Criticism* 62, no. 2 (Spring 2004): 141–152; and Marco Caracciolo, "Narrative, Meaning, Interpretation: An Enactivist Approach," *Phenomenology and the Cognitive Sciences* 11, no. 3 (2012) 367–384. A valuable essay collection is Meghan Marie Hammond and Sue J. Kim, eds. *Rethinking Empathy through Literature* (New York: Routledge, 2014).

empathic engagement or that invite empathic engagement that readers would condemn in real life. I suggest that texts that frustrate reader's empathy can beneficially expose limits in our capacity as lovers.

Two approaches to empathy

New technological developments in neuroimaging have made it possible for researchers to monitor readers' brain activity. Several experiments have been designed to determine to what extent the empathic reactions readers have toward characters resemble, and might therefore strengthen, the ability to have empathic reactions to real embodied others. Raymond Mar and Keith Oatley began theorizing that readers use stories as simulations of life at York University in 2006.[2] This has been confirmed in several functional magnetic resonance imaging (fMRI) studies since then. Researchers working at the Freie University of Berlin found that fear-inducing passages of *Harry Potter* ignited the same areas of readers' brains that are active when we empathize with someone's fear in person.[3] At Stanford, researchers discovered that in reading Jane Austen closely, "it was as though readers were physically placing themselves within the story as they analyzed it."[4] Neuroimaging has confirmed what attentive readers have long suspected—that readers perform the empathic action of putting themselves in another's place. Most of these experiments look only at the activation of an empathy network in the brain, but one experiment also measured participants' engagement in benevolent action after reading an empathy-inducing story. Dan Johnson, at Washington and Lee University, had a researcher drop some pens in sight of readers after

---

[2] Raymond A. Mar, Keith Oatley, Jacob Hirsh, Jennifer dela Paz, and Jordan B. Peterson, "Bookworms Versus Nerds: Exposure to Fiction versus Non-Fiction, Divergent Associations with Social Ability, and the Simulation of Fictional Social Worlds," *Journal of Research in Personality* 40, no. 5 (October 2006). Also, Raymond Mar and Keith Oatley, "The Function of Fiction is the Abstraction and Simulation of Social Experience," *Perspectives on Psychological Science* 3, no. 3 (2008).

[3] Chun-Ting Hsu, Markusa Conrad, and Arthur Jacobs, "Fiction Feelings in Harry Potter: Haemodynamic Response in the Mid-Cingulate Cortex Correlates with Immersive Reading Experience," *NeuroReport* 25, no. 17 (December 2014).

[4] Helen Thompsson and Shakar Vedantam, "A Lively Mind: Your Brain on Jane Austen," Morning Edition, *NPR* (16 October 2012). See Natalie Phillips's "Literary Neuroscience and the History of Attention: An fMRI Study of Reading Jane Austen," *The Oxford Handbook for Cognitive Approaches to Literature*, ed. Lisa Zunshine (Oxford: Oxford University Press, 2015).

they had read a story designed to encourage pro-social behavior. Johnson found that readers who had been more immersed in the story were more likely to help pick up the pens.[5] The wider availability of fMRI technology will create more opportunities for research like this to be performed, and the recent discovery of mirror neurons will facilitate research specifically directed toward reading's effect on the empathy network in the brain.

Suzanne Keen has performed the most exhaustive survey of neuroscientific findings about empathy relevant to reading. In her *Empathy and the Novel*, Keen draws on her knowledge of eighteenth- and nineteenth-century reading practices and the British discourses of empathy that developed alongside these to describe a history of perceptions of empathy and the novel. She then brings this history up to the present by investigating recent discoveries from the sociology and neuroscience of reading. The picture that emerges from her book is comprehensive and enlightening, but it is also a picture of a discipline looking everywhere but to the experience of daily life for evidence of empathy. Keen alludes to teaching as a site of empathic engagement in the everyday life of teachers and students, but her argumentative framework ultimately gives neuroscientific or quantitative sociological investigations more weight than her own teaching or reading experience. Keen's conclusion, alluded to in the "Interlude" of this volume, is that readers do experience empathy for fictional characters, but she also cautions that more empirical data is needed before we can conclude that reading novels makes people act more empathetically toward others in person. Keen recognizes that such evidence will be hard to obtain since actions inspired by empathy for another person always originate from a complex matrix of causes. She recommends longitudinal studies of novel readers as a way to overcome this difficulty.[6]

As helpful as Keen's book is for historicizing empathy and its relationship to reading, her call for empirical evidence seems to be a request for assurance where none can be found. If, for example, a scientist proved that a certain group of committed novel readers from a particular culture did indeed participate in community service more, then empathetic advocates for novel reading would

---

[5] Dan Johnson, "Transportation into a Story Increases Empathy, Prosocial Behavior, and Perceptual Bias toward Fearful Expressions," *Personality and Individual Differences* 52, no. 2 (2012): 150–155.

[6] Keen, *Empathy and the Novel*, 168.

cheer, but the results of such a study might obscure a cause of empathetic action more prior than novel reading. Perhaps those individuals studied had cultivated empathy through their relationships with others, and that led them to enjoy both the empathic expansion that novels offer and community service. There is no way to chart the development of an individual's empathetic capacity over the course of a life filled with the unpredictabilities of love and reading. The closest description of these complicated interactions will be a descriptive narrative created by the person living this relation—a memoir, or a phenomenological account.

A false sense of dependence on empirical evidence can hamper literary criticism. Thus, Keen and Ann Jurecic, another leading scholar working between neuropsychology and literary criticism, acknowledge that, in the end, brain images cannot tell a story themselves. They have to be situated within an already articulated theory of how what happens when we read connects with the rest of our lives. Jurecic concludes that the describing, enacting, and frustrating of empathy that readers find in literature attests to "the lived complexity of empathy" that "cannot be reduced to an outcome, 'a feeling,'" or "a neurological response."[7] If fMRI studies can reveal what is similar, neurologically, in two different experiences of empathy, it cannot capture the subtle differences that readers experience.

The other common approach to empathy within literary criticism asks what kinds of people a reader can feel empathy for most readily. Explicitly or implicitly, this vein of criticism separates categorical empathy from situational empathy. Categorical empathy is that which we experience for someone we perceive ourselves to share traits with. Situational empathy is that which we experience based on imagining what it would be like to face a scenario another person faces. From the eighteenth-century discussions of empathy until today, most scholars have agreed that we feel categorical empathy more readily. Reading, it is argued, better enables situational empathy by giving readers practice imagining another's situation.[8]

---

[7] Ann Jurecic, "Empathy and the Critic," *College English* 74, no. 1 (2011).
[8] For the terms *categorical empathy* and *situational empathy*, see Patrick Colm Hogan, "The Epilogue of Suffering: Heroism, Empathy, Ethics," *SubStance*, 30, nos. 1–2 (2001). He returns to these issues in his later *Affective Narratology: The Emotional Structure of Stories* (Lincoln: University of Nebraska Press, 2011), especially the afterward, 237–251.

One advocate for literature who relies on this ontology is Martha Nussbaum, whose *Cultivating Humanity*, now almost twenty years old, remains a powerful articulation of literature's role in one's becoming a compassionate person. Nussbaum believes in literature's ability to strengthen readers in the power of empathy, but she implies a fundamental isolation of individuals. For her, squarely within the natural attitude, we are isolated by our bodies from one another and sortable like so many clothes. While containing some combination of the same materials, readers can be divided into color, size, gender, and use. "Compassion requires demarcations," she writes. A reader can compassionately imagine himself as someone from another class or nation because one could feasibly change from being rich to being poor or could move from one nation to another. "Boundaries of race, of gender, and of sexual orientation prove, historically, more recalcitrant: for there might appear to be little real-life possibility of a man becoming a woman, a white person's becoming black, or even (pace earlier psychiatry) a straight person's becoming gay or lesbian."[9] Her goal here is positive and liberating. If a reader cannot change his skin color, he can "imagine what it is like to inhabit a race different from one's own," and become more compassionate through that imaginary act. But Nussbaum's line of thought implies that a certain set of thinking patterns, feelings, and modes of perception adheres to each side of the blackness/whiteness, masculinity/femininity, gay/straight dichotomies at an ontological level. Moreover, it occludes the otherness of people who physically resemble us.

Not only have these specific dichotomies come under scrutiny in the last twenty years, the process of slotting people into categorizable traits is problematic from the beginning.[10] Even if a scholar takes great care to make

---

[9] Martha Nussbaum, *Cultivating Humanity: A Classical Defense of Reform in Liberal Education* (Cambridge: Harvard University Press, 1997), 92.

[10] Other critics, referenced below, have also pointed out problems with the ontological implications of identity categorization whether it is based on biological or socially deterministic categories. These accounts challenging such categorization indicate the extent to which ontological claims still underlie criticism associated with ethnicity, gender, and queer studies. Ontological determinism persists in applied literary criticism in spite of, more than because of, theoretical speculations about the issue. See Mari Mikkola, "Ontological Commitments, Sex and Gender," in *Feminist Metaphysics: Explorations in the Ontology of Sex, Gender and the Self*, ed. Charlotte Witt (New York: Springer), 67–83; Homi Bhabha, *Location of Culture*, 2nd edition (London: Routledge, 2012), especially the conclusion, 338–367; and Malena Gustavson, "Bisexuals in Relationships: Uncoupling Intimacy from Gender Ontology," *Bisexual and Queer Theory: Intersections, Connections and Challenges*, eds. Jonathan Alexander and Serena Anderlini-D'Onofrio (London: Routledge, 2014), 215–237.

these traits flexible and subtly graded, such a conception of selfhood can never account for the complexity of what we are. If imagination is to be the bridge that stretches between me and the fictional or actual other, then I need to imagine myself not merely as a member of some other category (black, male, rich) as though those were stable drawings on a sidewalk that I could just step into and become part of. These categories are not only socially adaptable, they are endlessly adapted by individuals moving daily between separate micro-cultures. Who is to say which categories of identity will be privileged as facilitating identification in which moment of a particular interaction? No amount of nuance will slot any imagined or actual individual into a category that preexisted their coming to be. What category could contain the bell hooks that emerges from her essays in *Belonging: A Culture of Place*? What matrix of traits could describe Tess Durbeyfield? Or Jakob Beer, of *Fugitive Pieces*, languishing among unplayed piano sonatas? Every person in the flesh, and every literary character worthy of the name adds something unforeseen to the world. Reading offers a privileged opportunity to engage empathetically with an other without the illusion of autonomy that bodily distance and difference creates. What is needed then, for an understanding of empathy's action in literature and life, is an ontology that presumes both the uniqueness and the potential interconnectedness of every individual. I say "potential" not because we are not already intersubjectively formed, but because each new person we meet can form us anew.

There are two problems that persist in discussions of literature and empathy, one of which is recognized, and the other that hides. First, in importing a model of empathy from psychology and neuroscience, some literary critics have separated the cognitive and affective elements of empathy. These can be separated for the sake of analytical discussion or brain-mapping, but they cannot be separated in any description that accords with the lived experience of empathy. The processes empathy is reported to include have been variously distinguished, but a fairly common division is between "primitive empathy" and the more cognitive "perspective taking." Babies, it is often pointed out, cry when they hear other babies cry. That is primitive empathy. Perspective taking is the process of imagining what a situation looks like from another's viewpoint. Sometimes primitive empathy is associated with emotional contagion, which is distinguished from a more distanced feeling-for, but not with, another person. However, when most adults experience empathy for another person they are from the first doing more than the sum of a primitive feeling-with or the more advanced feeling-for the other and perspective taking. When a lover sees her beloved in distress, something more overpowering than either feeling-for or feeling-with happens from the very beginning even if there is no simultaneous "perspective taking" contemplation about what may have caused the distress. The problem of the initial separation of affect and cognition has been lost in the proposed solution or re-attending to affect.

The other problem, which is very much in the open and motivates much empathy-oriented criticism, is the problem of connecting an experience of empathy to action that tries to protect another's joyful experience or mediate a painful one. Here, too, it might be advantageous to rejoin two elements that have been analyzed apart, in this case being and doing. A discourse of empathy that relies too heavily on ontology will argue (as Nussbaum does) that reading can strengthen our habits of compassionate imagination and, by facilitating this improvement to a capacity latent in our being, facilitate empathetic action. In this case, it is the consistency of an individual that binds the action of reading to the action of helping another. If this basis of consistency disappears entirely, and the ego is imagined as only the retrospectively imagined sum of what one does, then there remains no consistent basis to bind the act of reading to a later act of empathy.

Empathy, phenomenology, and literature

Phenomenological considerations of empathy can redirect literary critical speculations about whether empathy encourages altruistic actions by examining empathy not as an act, but as a fundamental human condition. They can reconfigure questions of affective versus cognitive empathy by approaching empathy as a kind of intentionality. Max Scheler, a prolific German phenomenologist who intrigued and sometimes challenged Husserl, offers a model of empathy that escapes the being/doing divide and resists the imposition of a cause-effect-interpretation chronology that some other theories of empathy imply. He wrote in his 1913 *Formalism in Ethics* that "the whole person is contained in every fully concrete act, and the whole person 'varies' in and through every act."[11] If someone cries, reaches out a hand, or smiles, these acts make that person present to us in a forceful way that is neither emotional contagion nor a cognitivist reconstruction of imagined emotions. Through an empathetic engagement with that person, the lover (which we all are) enables both whole people involved to "vary" and emerge more fully. Instead of dividing empathy into logical or emotional acts that begin from an assumption of distance between subjects, phenomenologists have instead worked to describe empathy as a "unique and irreducible form of intentionality" that is called forth by the moment.[12] What each beloved gives the other in this moment, even in a simple smile, is more than the intention of either could contain. Although empathy may be followed by reflection, it does not depend on it. It is not a step-by-step process, but occurs all at once.

Because another person offers an endless hermeneutic, a person receiving a smile may speculate what that smile meant and what prompted it, but inferring a logically constructible chronology of cause, effect (smile), and signification posits a mechanistic process of human relating that does not adequately describe what happens when we smile at each other. The togetherness of an emphatic moment, such as sharing a smile, differentiates it from a moment of perceiving an object. Togetherness, in this case, does not mean simply a temporal-spatial coincidence, as in "here we are in this room together," but suggests a condition of possibility. The immediate possibility of perceiving something together with someone else differs from seeing that same thing alone. If a person sees a sycamore in winter, she knows that it is available for the perception of many others, even if she is alone. However, when she looks at a sycamore in winter and experiences it as beautiful and turns to her beloved and smiles, his returning smile is not available to others in the way that the tree is. It is just for her. Even more precisely, she and her lover smile together.

---

[11] Max Scheler, *Formalism in Ethics and Non-Formal Ethics of Values: A New Attempt Toward the Foundation of an Ethical Personalism*, trans. Manfred Frings and Robert L. Funk (Evanston, IL: Northwestern University Press, 1973), 384.

[12] Dan Zahavi, "Beyond Empathy: Phenomenological Approaches to Intersubjectivity," *Journal of Consciousness Studies* 8, nos. 5–7 (2001): 151–167. While Zahavi's article has helped me clarify a phenomenological view of empathy, he critiques the "empathic approach" that he defines with this phrase.

That empathetic act of smiling together draws into itself three realms of phenomenological perception often discussed separately—the life world, intersubjectivity, and intentionality.[13] The tree is given in the world, but also simultaneously in a world colored by the beloved's presence. It is, for the man in this example, the tree-in-the-way-I-know-she-would-see-it-and-find-it-beautiful, at the same time as it is the tree itself for him, perhaps an unremarkable tree. The man's smile arises as the expression of that act of seeing-as-the-lover-sees. It is a gift for the beloved, uniquely brought forth by her as she is a part of him, but not dependent on her immediate presence. He might have smiled to see the tree as she would see it even if she were not there. But if he directs the smile to her, if he intends her and she perceives herself seen, then her reception of his act of seeing-as-she-sees will be offered back in her returning smile. This kind of empathetic engagement is not the only form of love, or the only form of intersubjectivity, but it is an important one. Phenomenological descriptions of such acts of empathy seem to be unique in their recognition of the at-once-ness of empathic intentionality—how it takes in something seen, the beloved's way of seeing, the lover's act of seeing with what I describe in Chapter 3 as double vision, and the beloved's seeing all of this in her lover's smile, all at once. The word "simultanneity" would not be accurate because it would imply separate actions sharing a temporal space. These acts of seeing overlap and depend on each other more than that.

My description of an empathetic act includes an external referent, the tree, but empathy does not depend on a visible referent to occur. Empathic intentionality is only a kind of willingness to see, be seen by, and see with another person. If I find my lover suddenly crying, the cause may be a mystery to one or both of us. If I catch the eye of a flustered father on the bus or a harried waitress or an old woman watching the sea, I may engage that person with empathy and find my gaze welcomed and overwhelmed without ever knowing what preceded the fluster, the harried manner or the patient watching. Other

---

[13] I use "life world" here as defined by Husserl in *The Crisis of the European Sciences and Transcendental Phenomenology*, trans. David Carr (Evanston, IL: Northwestern University Press, 1970), 108: "In whatever way we may be conscious of the world as universal horizon, as coherent universe of existing objects, we, each "I-the-man" and all of us together, belong to the world as living with one another in the world; and the world is our world, valid for our consciousness as existing precisely through this 'living together.' "

acts (helping the father with his shopping bags) may or may not follow that moment of empathy, but the empathy itself is not somehow annulled if nothing else follows. I am not suggesting that it would be ethically conscionable to empathize with someone needing help and then not help, but the singularity of situations between people would introduce a great many more questions. (Would it be helpful for the waitress in the long run if I cleared her tables for her?) For an investigation into empathy's role in love and reading, the focus must remain initially on empathy as a kind of intentionality.

Phenomenologists have debated whether intersubjectivity arises from or precedes encounters with others. Intersubjectivity cannot be said to exist outside of the myriad relationships that develop and change between people, but there is never a time for any person when love or its absence cannot be said to have made and sustained him or her. Empathy, therefore, arises out of an intersubjectivity that conditions all of our lives; it does not give rise to it. Lévinas and Marion have provided the clearest articulations of a human intersubjective connection prior to the ego's self-awareness, but phenomenology has been suspicious of the autonomous self from its very beginnings.[14] Husserl wondered if "when empathy occurs, is perhaps community, intersubjectivity, likewise already there, and does empathy then merely accomplish the disclosure of it?"[15] Elsewhere Husserl is more inclined to see the Ego as surrounded by other isolated egos who share a world and forms of understanding with it,[16] but throughout his writing the sense that the Ego is always enmeshed with other egos returns, as when he describes an "intersubjective nexus" already in place that facilitates "intersubjective identification."[17]

Heidegger uses a book to illustrate the way that our engagement with things is also an engagement with other people. A book we read "was bought at So-and-so's shop and given by such-and-such a person." Things carry with them, as it were, the past or potential future actions of other people. By "others" Heidegger does not mean "those over against whom the 'I' stands out," but

---

[14] "Intersubjective" is not an accurate term to use when discussing Marion since he does not accept that there is a subject, but I use the term to convey the intertwining of selves within the erotic reduction.

[15] Quoted in Zahavi, "Beyond Empathy," 156, from an unpublished manuscript in the Husserl Archives (C 17 84b).

[16] Husserl, *Ideas*, 55 and 93.

[17] Husserl, *Ideas*, 92.

those "from whom, for the most part, one does not distinguish oneself." Nevertheless, Heidegger finds that the entity of "Dasein," or being, "is unrelated to Others" existentially and comes to be " 'with' Others afterwards."[18] For him, and for Husserl at times, the self begins alone and enters into communal selfhood through actions such as empathy, communication, or sharing things. For Marion and Lévinas, we are as we are through others always. For Marion, we arrive as children already constituted in love, and the moving forward which is life is always sustained by love or the hope of it. Lévinas has done more than any modern philosopher to draw attention to the fundamental interconnectedness each of us abides in. Every person engages the face of every other responsible for that other and dependent on him for self-enaction.

Marion's erotic reduction relies more heavily on Lévinasian ontology than he often admits. Marion follows Lévinas in his articulation of our already-togetherness with other people, but he distances himself from Lévinas's use of the Other. For him, what matters to us in love is this other, this particular other who I have loved first and explained my love for afterwards. We do have a responsibility, as Lévinas indicates, to extend our love first to each other we meet, only after, if we must, trying to give ourselves a reason for having loved this other. But the recipient of our love is always a particular man, woman, or child in Marion's formulation. The givenness of intersubjectivity still precedes being, but there is no existent web of interrelationality that precedes individual acts of love. We depend on these acts. We could not exist without them, but we have to make them. This difference in whether intersubjectivity precedes or follows a person's experience of himself as a self is important for considering empathy's role in reading.

Because every reader is always intersubjectively brought forth into the world and is never disentangled from the loves and hates of other people, the empathy a reader feels for a character is also already tied to other people. A reader who has loved a soldier cannot read *The Sun Also Rises* as though she had not known one. Conversely, if a woman comes to love a soldier while reading Hemingway's novel, she cannot somehow tear the world of the book out of her while engaging her new love. Whatever might enable or block a

[18] Heidegger, *Being and Time*, 154–156.

reader's empathy with *The Sun Also Rises*, he or she experiences that empathy as someone entwined in past and present loves. The operation of empathy in a novel does not proceed according to an ethical rule, but only as a new act of love, and only in a way that was possible for one specific reader in her specific temporal-spatial and cultural location. Unique as empathic acts are, invitations to empathic action can be discerned in works of literature. These invitations emerge from texts, so they maintain independence from the reader, but they also only come forth through her engagement with a work. In the following section, I investigate the way one novel, *Fugitive Pieces*, invites empathy.

Fugitive Pieces

Anne Michaels's *Fugitive Pieces* is composed on two parts. The first part, about twice as long as the second, tells the story of Jakob Beer, a Polish-Jewish boy whose family is taken away during World War II while he hides behind a wall. He escapes to Greece with the help of Athos Roussos, a scholar moving between archeology and geology, in Jakob's words "an expert in buried and abandoned places."[19] The first section takes the form of Jakob's diary. Jakob becomes a poet, as Michaels herself is, and the language in this section of the book is richly textured. The second part of the novel contains the first person narration of a character named Ben, a young professor at the University of Toronto where Jakob and Athos move after the war. He goes to the island in Greece where Jakob had lived with his Toronto wife Michaela to recover Jakob's journals after he and Michaela have died.

The first part is full of half-accomplished books. Athos longs to complete *Bearing False Witness*, about the bog people of Biskupin whose sophisticated civilization the Nazis tried to erase from history. He dies before it is completed, and Jakob completes it from notes. Jakob's own books of poetry are written "askew" because he feels his "life could not be stored in any language but only in silence" (111). Sometimes years pass between the gaps in the paragraphs of the journal we imagine we are reading, and the entire section in Jakob's voice never

---

[19] Anne Michaels, *Fugitive Pieces* (London: Bloomsbury, 1997), 49. Cited hereafter in the text.

quite makes it into present tense. "Every moment is two moments"; the debris of life in the present recalls some partially hidden instance from the past. The founding gesture of the novel alludes to unfinished tales of unfinished lives that remain hidden and unread. At the beginning, before the pages are numbered, there is a page reporting that during World War II, "countless manuscripts— diaries, memoirs, eyewitness accounts—were lost or destroyed." This is a fact. Michaels creates Jakob's story out the rich lives that she can imagine having been lost, embedding within the novel small stories from history containing lives that readers are invited to imagine themselves: the forgotten history of the Jews of Corfu, for example, or the village of Kalavrita.

The second part of the book focuses on what can and cannot be seen more than on text and silence. Ben is the child of two Holocaust survivors. In their lives "every thing belonged to, had been retrieved from, impossibility" (205). Ben knows his parents' stories through "strange episodic images" (216). The image that almost bursts through the pages is one he finds after his parents have died, a snapshot of his parents before the war. His father bears an infant in one arm and encourages a little girl with the other (252). Ben never knew there had been other children. These images impose the same weight as the unwritten stories of the book's first section. The shadow of what cannot be seen or cannot be written hovers over the entire novel, and this is what makes its analysis in terms of empathy so fruitful. As Ben stares at faces in a magazine, he expresses an injunction that becomes the reader's injunction: "It was my responsibility to imagine who they might be" (221). This evocation of responsibility could almost have almost been spoken by Lévinas, who writes that "the responsibility for the Other, being-for-the-other, … stop[s] the anonymous and senseless rumbling of being" and replaces it with love.[20]

The book won the Orange Prize for Fiction in 1997, was a best seller in Canada, the United States and the United Kingdom, and was reissued in paperback in 2009. The large pool of readers that these accolades imply, must contain some with personal ties to the histories that form the book's background, but most readers will have little basis for categorical empathy

[20] Emmanuel Lévinas, *Ethics and Infinity: Conversations with Philippe Nemo*, trans. Richard Cohen (Pittsburgh: Duquesne University Press, 1985), 52. Lévinas states here that the word love is "compromised," and in doing so suggests that it is the idea if not the word that he wants.

with the characters. It would be inadequate to explain empathy's function in the novel through the analogical process implied by situational empathy, too. Raymond Mar and Keith Oatley, researchers whose work on the cognitive science of reading was mentioned earlier, write that "to the psychologist, fictional literature offers a site of scenarios that can be both experienced and potentially understood."[21] This cognitivist approach to reading initially seem sensible, but when thinking about the scenarios described in *Fugitive Pieces*, it becomes clear that readers can quite precisely *not* experience and *not* understand what Jakob and Ben suffer. One does not imagine oneself in Jakob Beer's place. The force of his implied past on the character's description of his present and the dense, often metaphorical prose used for his narration reinforces the uniqueness of Jakob's manner of experiencing his life with every page. Jakob's manner of describing his experience reminds readers how strange any other must be to us even with less remarkable life circumstances. Our responsibility as readers is not to imagine our life via a novel, thereby instrumentalizing the implied voice of another person. It is to imagine "who they might be."

Fugitive Pieces models several ways of performing that kind of empathic act, leading the reader in acts of empathy, but it also shows empathy's limits. These limits are not a failing of empathy, but an exposure of what it really is. As a kind of intentionality, empathy succeeds to the extent that it provides space for the other to give him or herself. Its success should not be judged by one's ability to imagine the experience of the other because to do so too fully would be to block the givenness of the other person through anticipation. Insofar as the imagination of who the other might be opens up a space for their experience to become the object of the lover's receptive intentional empathy, then to that extent empathy has managed to join the empathizer and the empathized-with in love. With a character in a book, the holes in a narrative remind us of all we cannot know about anyone. With a grandfather, a spouse, a quiet child, we can ask to have these holes filled in, a luxury we do not enjoy with fictional characters. That lack of possibility in books can reawaken readers to the possibility of trying to fill these gaps in person. They never are filled in

---

[21] Mar and Oatley, "Function of Fiction," 187.

because they are not exactly holes that inscribe a space to be filled in. We are more dynamic than such a spatial metaphor implies. It is the narrativization of a person's experience that makes what remains invisible of a person appear as a gap. In wondering about these gaps, we create space for our embodied beloveds to come forth in person, in love.

Several characters model empathy in the novel. Since Jakob and Ben focalize the narrative, their ways of seeing are more explicitly explored. In one case, Jakob listens to the story of the Hania (Chania) ghetto on Crete whose population was evacuated by boat. He writes that "the room filled with shouts" as Ioannis, the storyteller spoke. "The water" within the story "rose around" the listeners, "bullets tearing the surface for those who took too long to drown" (43). This instance of extreme identification with the victims is pictured as being shared by every listener of the story ("the water rose around *us*"). Michaels evokes a powerful image of empathy—drowning in another's experience—but by giving the empathic act symbolic significance, she also reminds readers of the fact that, for us, the incident occurs via a symbolic medium. The story we drown in can be put away. Seawater cannot. In realizing that the water readers imagine sinking in lacks the materiality of that which surrounded those from the boat and lacks the sense of engulfment that overtakes the traumatized Jakob, we see the extent to which we can never share another's experience, as well as the importance of preserving the narrative shell that testifies to that absence.

The failure of empathy

Fugitive Pieces guides readers in capacious empathic intentionality even as it overwhelms that intentionality with an implied vastness of experience that we cannot take in. Some texts, however, frustrate empathy from the start, or invite empathic reading that draws readers into mental acts closer to hate than love. I will close this chapter by considering these failures of empathy. Since literature does call to us, and I am arguing that this call resembles the call to love that another person gives us, it would be easy to infer that readers should answer all calls. We should react with vulnerability to the call a book issues.

We should be open to being changed. But of course, sometimes answering the call of a book is not possible. Sometimes it is not desirable. Gadamer praises literature's ability to make us aware of the shape of our own prejudices and its ability to draw us toward another, broader, potentially more ethically desirable horizon. Certainly literature can work this way, but it would be naïve to suppose that it always does.

The novel's success in giving rise to empathy has led to questions about whether expending empathy on fictional characters fosters or fatigues real-world empathy. History attests to the banal, evil actions of people whose reading habits would indicate a ready capacity to step into someone else's story. A reader who has no recognition of his dependence on love may read with no attention to or even to distract himself from the needs of real people. I have alluded already to George Steiner's lifelong concern that "what man has inflicted on man" has permanently affected the humanistic argument for reading that reigned "from the time of Plato to that of Matthew Arnold." "Not only did the general dissemination of literary, cultural values prove no barrier to totalitarianism; but in notable instances, the high places of humanistic learning and art actually welcomed and aided the new terror."[22] Recent history's testimony against the perseverance of empathy within a culture that does not support it cannot be ignored, but the painful fact that reading has failed to make some people more empathetic does not negate all those instances in which people have matured as empathizers through reading.

The empathy we feel for characters is clean, simple, and controllable in a way that empathizing in person is sometimes not. This difference might account for some people's ability to empathize with literary characters more easily than with other real, embodied others. For example, Jakob seems poetic, vulnerable, and utterly worth protecting when he emerges from a Polish forest filthy and inarticulate. But, the filth that suggests a universally shared material body in a novel might seem merely like filth in person. The inarticulateness that suggests unnamable suffering might, in person. disable empathy and encourage condescension. As Keen argues, skepticism and self-protection operate more readily in real life than in fiction and can stifle empathy.

---

[22] George Steiner, *Language and Silence: Essays on Language, Literature and the Inhuman* (New Haven: Yale University Press, 1998), 5.

Literature cannot overcome this in individuals who, because of social pressure or habitual callousness, block the flow of empathy between themselves and another person, but for those who already value empathy, literature can strengthen the function of empathic intentionality.

Reading within the erotic reduction, we encounter the opposite problem of empathizing too much. Marion bids us as lovers to open ourselves unconditionally, in all hope, to what countering signification may offer us. If literature has the power to strengthen readers as lovers in this process, then it also has the power to strengthen us in hate. The poetry used in terrorist recruiting has this as its goal, as did Hitler's *Mein Kampf*.[23] Perhaps it is not surprising that literature's stimulation of hateful emotions has received less attention than its encouragement of fellow feeling. A comparison with some video games or TV serials makes the violence novels might provoke us to imagine seem mild. But the process of that imagining calls for more engaged intentionality in the case of literature. Cormac McCarthy's *Blood Meridian* offers a provocative example of a novel that makes readers complicit with evil for the sake of exposing that complicity. The evil it provokes is not empathy with the criminals that roam its pages, but rather the failure of empathy. The distance between McCarthy's narrator and the violent characters creates a paradox for the reader. We are directed to ask what it is in us that would seek closer identification with these characters and led ultimately to resign ourselves to empathy's failure. Without being able to understand the characters' motives or to imagine how they experience their lives, readers must accept a spectator position and encounter the novel's violence as aesthetic, but the magnitude of that violence consistently reminds readers of the consequences of failing to empathize.

Based on the bounty-hunting Glanton gang, McCarthy's characters distinguish themselves in their creative brutality. Exceeding them all is Judge Holden, a seven-foot-tall, hairless genius who enacts and at one point paraphrases what Hannah Arendt defines as the totalitarian maxim: everything is possible.[24] The first time the reader encounters him, the Judge convinces the

---

[23] For an overview of the use of poetry to motivate terrorist acts, see William Yeldham, "Culturally Combatting ISIS," *The Spectrum* (26 August 2015).

[24] Cormac McCarthy, *Blood Meridian* (Basingstoke: Picador, 1990), 256. Hereafter cited in the text. Hannah Arendt, *The Origins of Totalitarianism* (New York: Harcourt, Brace Jovanovich, 1973), 438.

congregation at a revival meeting that the preacher has raped an eleven-year-old girl and a goat, and they rise and beat him to death. The Judge immediately is tied to an act that displays his own lack of empathy and exposes the violent capacity within everyone. Throughout the novel, he finds bits of departed human settlements and draws them in a sketchbook before destroying them (147). Webster, one of the Glanton men, praises the Judge's skill as a draughtsman but remarks that "no man can put all the world in a book. No more than everything drawed in a book is so" (148). The Judge contests this, saying that "What is to be deviates no jot from the book wherin its writ." *Blood Meridian* thus claims through the Judge to inscribe "what is to be," which gives its violence disturbing resonance and claim to universality.

Equally disturbing is another comment that the Judge makes just after: "Whether in my book or not, every man is tablernacled in every other and he in exchange and so on in an endless complexity of being and witness to the uttermost edge of the world" (148). The verb "to tabernacle" comes from a direct English translation of verse 1:14 in the Gospel of John, which reads, "And the word became flesh and did tabernacle among us, and we beheld his glory."[25] The verb entered English as a translation of this verse in 1653 according the Oxford English Dictionary, and after a small revival of use in the nineteenth century, mostly in devotional literature, disappeared again. McCarthy's use of this unique word suggests both the sacredness of everyone's dwelling in and becoming through the other (as in Lévinas), and also the dissolution of the sacred, the replacement of the inimitable divine presence in each person with the presence of other human beings who, in the Judge's logic, can be "exchanged." He acknowledges an endless complexity of being, as such, but not the complexity or sacredness of specific beings. When Webster addresses him, the Judge has just drawn a foot guard "from a suit of armor hammered out in a shop in Toledo three centuries before." After drawing it, he tosses it into the fire. This action indicates that the copy will do well enough to replace the real thing. If every man contains a copy of every other and those copies are exchangeable, then men, like the armor created to protect them, can be crumpled and tossed away. The superfluity of violence in

---

[25] *Young's Literal Translation of the Holy Bible* (Oxford: Benedictine Classics, 2012).

the book shows how readily men are tossed away—in the mid 1800s when the book is set, three centuries before that in Toledo when the armor was deemed necessary, and before and after and now. The book is full of unnamed and exchangeable men and more exchangeable women. "The kid" becomes "the man" but never a specific man with a personal name. Two characters with the same name are differentiated only by their race—the black Jackson and the white Jackson. They demonstrate their ability to cancel each other out when one kills the other.

The book's lack of individuation coupled with extreme violence implies a conclusion that psychologist Simon Baron-Cohen has also come to—that an inability or unwillingness to empathize with another person is where evil starts.[26] This is also the conclusion of phenomenologist and political philosopher Hannah Arendt. The Judge in fact hypostasizes totalitarian evil according to her definition. Totalitarianism seeks to show that everything is possible. McCarthy has the Judge say this at one point: "The truth about the world, he said, is that anything is possible." If we forget it, that is because we have "seen it all from birth and thereby bled it of its strangeness" (258). The dissolution of all moral bounds, the evacuation of the holy from the man tabernacled in every other, clears the way for what Arendt calls "the absolute evil." Her image for this evil is the image of substitutable persons: "Murder in the camp is as impersonal as the squashing of a gnat."[27] Evil is "closely connected with the invention of a system in which all men are equally superfluous."

Empathy rejects the idea that people are superfluous and must equally reject the idea that they are exchangeable. Books, viewed from within the erotic reduction, do not invite us to imagine ourselves in another's position. Such substitution of persons is impossible, and the implications of substitutability are violent. Rather, books invite us to try to see, feel, and otherwise experience the other's lifeworld as he or she experiences it, while recognizing that our empathic intentionality can never contain another's experience. *Fugitive Pieces* guides readers in empathic intentionality and in moments of philosophical

---

[26] Simon Baron-Cohen, *The Science of Evil: On Empathy and the Origins of Cruelty* (Philadelphia: Basic Books, 2012), 15.

[27] Quoted from the first edition of *The Human Condition* in Richard J. Bernstein, *Hannah Arendt and the Jewish Question* (Cambridge: Polity Press, 1996), 139. Arendt dropped part of her "Concluding Remarks" from editions after 1958.

reflection outrightly advocates for it, but through the recurrence of images suggesting unseen life and texts that fail to voice another's suffering, it thematizes empathy's limits. *Blood Meridian*, in contrast, dramatizes what happens when the substitution of one man for another is taken as possible. The Kid, the book's protagonist, contests this by continuing to individualize the other characters in the story even in the midst of his own violence. The extreme lack of empathy in much of the novel draws attention to its absence and posits violence as that which fills the vacuum left behind. Formally, the book frustrates empathy by failing to individualize or blocking access to characters. By immersing readers in an environment that devalues empathy, the novel tests readers' capacity to sustain empathic intentionality.

In the next chapter I turn from a specific form of intentionality to attention itself suggesting that the self-forgetting form of attention reading calls us to is central to love as well as reading. Empathic reading, as part of the lover's advance discussed in the last chapter, immerses me in "the alterity of the other" who is "unsubstitutable" and precious even when, like the Judge or (less problematically) the Kid, that other exemplifies a failure of empathy in him or herself. Because books have no potential to intend their readers, they provide a unique opportunity to empathize without hope of return. Empathic intentionality relies on the broader practice of attending to something outside oneself. Lévinas states that "the forgetting of self moves justice."[28] Likewise it moves love.

---

[28] Lévinas, *Otherwise than Being*, 159.

5

Attention

Describing the adonné, the receiver of gifts that we all are, Thomas Carlson writes:

> If everything is given and the given is without limit or reserve, every moment gives something utterly new—unforeseen and unforeseeable— and thus always still to be seen, and the obligation of the adonné in every moment is to decide, without ground, to receive and to see what gives itself by responding to it and so making it phenomenal.[1]

According to this formulation, our greatest responsibility is to pay attention. The phenomenological reduction places this responsibility upon us because it is only through our attention that events (including events of reading) can be phenomenalized. The erotic reduction enforces the responsibility to pay attention even further. It is through the attentions of others that we are formed in love, so conversely it is through attending to another person in love that we help him or her come forth as a person.

The attention that the lover gives another person is not the attention that she gives an object because her beloved is not phenomenologically separable from her. Marion, like Lévinas, sees the ego as always in relation to others and always entangled with previous loves and hates as it engages a new other. "Moral consciousness," as Lévinas says, is "not a modality of psychological

---

[1] Thomas A. Carlson, "Blindness and the Decision to See: On Revelation and Reception in Jean-Luc Marion," *Counter-Experiences*, ed. Kevin Hart (Notre Dame, IN: Notre Dame University Press, 2007), 168.

consciousness, but its condition."[2] Similarly, it might be said for Marion that love is not a mode of consciousness, but its very source. The question of intentionality, of how we attend to things, must take account of the self's already givenness in love because the attention we give to other people does not originate with the lover, but is called forth by the other with whom I am bound in love. Although a reader bears no moral responsibility for the book he opens, the attention he gives a book similarly originates in the book's invitation to him. Because books reach us as saturated phenomena, inviting us to attend to them in a particular way and then overwhelming our intentionality, they have a capacity to change us that resembles the capacity of another person. Turning away from a book does not amount to a denial of a summons at an ontological level as turning away from a person does, but at the point that we allow a book to engage our attention, we find that the intentionality we turn to it is shaped from the very first moment by the kind of summons that the book itself issues. We relax into a book's shape as we read, recognizing that the attention we pay to it and the attention that it bids us to pay to the rest of the world change constantly and without the domination of our will. At the moment we begin to pay attention to a book it engages our attention in much the same way that a person does. In directing reader's attention, literature helps us to forget ourselves. Literature's ability to encourage self-forgetfulness is important within the erotic reduction because self-forgetfulness is a conditional requirement for fully receptive attention.

Texts both direct and receive attention, and both of these operations need to be theorized. In his introduction to the *Oxford Handbook of Philosophy and Literature*, Richard Eldridge suggests that literature and philosophy are themselves modes of attention, and that these modes can be further divided into generically categorizable acts—lyric poetry as a mode of attention in literature, for instance, or a treatise as a mode of attention in philosophy. Eldridge's notion of generic modes of attention could be carried even further to say that individual texts operate as different modes of giving attention. Kevin Hart has made this suggestion in phenomenological terms. He suggests

---

[2] Emmanuel Lévinas, "Signature," ed. Adrian Peperzak, *Research in Phenomenology* 8 (January 1978): 183.

that every literary text operates as its own phenomenological reduction.[3] Such miniature reductions do not make permanent, totalizing claims on readers in the way that a Husserelian, Heideggerian, or Marionian reduction does, but thinking of a text as a reduction does capture the way that a poem or novel can radically reshape a reader's means of paying attention.

It is not just that a work of literature can make visible something a reader would otherwise not have seen, but also that the work organizes the time a reader spends attending to that newly visible thing. As Ricoeur notes, it is temporality that most clearly connects our engagement with our remembered life and our engagement with other stories, those belonging to real others and fictional others. The "common feature of human experience, that which is marked, organized, and clarified by storytelling in all its forms, is its temporal character."[4] However much we may or may not contemplate them afterwards, readers will pay attention to dolls for fifty lines in chapter 1 of Toni Morrison's *The Bluest Eye*. Later, they will anticipate Aunt Jimmy's death by peach cobbler from pages 106 to 109.[5] Even the most unimaginative reader experiences some self-forgetfulness in the face of Aunt Jimmy's death. Comprehension alone requires this. The degree to which we forget ourselves and the degree to which a work controls a reader's attention temporally varies depending on both textual and readerly factors. A work establishes its own norms, for density of language, pace of plot, level of realism, extent of reflection, and so on, and awakens greater attention from readers by deviating from the norms it has set. The absurdity of Aunt Jimmy's mode of demise in a realistic book provokes more detailed attention than a more predictable cause of death might have.

Beyond the contemplation of peach cobbler, the question of what individual readers will pay attention to becomes more complicated. Morrison's portrayal of Aunt Jimmy's death may *invite* us to attend to her experience by imagining various physical sensations or by reflecting on what a good death might be, but readers may accept or reject that invitation to varying degrees. In reading, the happenstance of a reader's spatio-temporal existence, particularly the past

---

[3] Hart, "It/Is True," 224.

[4] Paul Ricoeur, *From Text to Action: Essays in Hermeneutics II*, trans. Katherine Blamey and John B. Thompson (New York: Continuum, 2008), 2.

[5] Toni Morrison, *The Bluest Eye* (London: Vintage, 1999).

experiences that are or are not available for imaginative attention, combine with the specificity of a text to limit the possibilities of readerly attention. These limits may be generative, in the way that meter can be generative for a poet's creation, but they are limits nonetheless. For example, the description of Aunt Jimmy's death includes experiences that readers of varying backgrounds will conjure with varying degrees of accuracy. I can well imagine that some academic proponents of Morrison have no personal experience with pot liquor. A reader may not be *able* to accept the text's invitation to recall the taste of pot liquor. Not having the intuition of pot liquor available while reading will limit a reader's ability to attend to the local medicine woman's prescription that Aunt Jimmy "drink pot liquor and nothing else" to overcome her illness. Surely, having tasted pot liquor will affect a reader's reception of the information that Aunt Jimmy accepted some peach cobbler against the doctor's orders. To some extent then, the way a text directs our attention to the world is always structured by the experience that we can bring to the text, and we are only partially in control of the experiences we have. Our intentionality reflects from the very beginning what the world has given to us and what the book gives us. Thus there are some elements of attention that can be described but not controlled.

Readers can exert more control, however, over the way that they unite their experience with a text in the act of reading. Put simply, a reader can *try* to accept a text's invitation to imagine and reflect on certain things in certain ways. Describing the older black women who tend Aunt Jimmy during her illness, Morrison writes, "The legs that straddled a mule's back were the same ones that straddled their men's hips. And the difference was all the difference there was." Full stop. End of paragraph. The text invites the reader to spend time thinking about the difference mentioned here. But the text cannot command the reader's reflection after the words have sounded in her head.

The theorization of texts' power of directing readers' attention must, therefore, be complemented by a theorization of the kind of attention readers can give to a text. When we pay attention in reading, what exactly do we pay attention to? In Chapter 2, I introduced the concept of imaginative variation, the practice of walking through different possible interpretations of a work of literature in order to explore the boundaries of the work's interpretive range. Such an exercise involves paying attention to different facets of a work alternatively, staying with each one to see what insights it produces. It is an act of reading *with* a text—not rewriting as Stanley Fish would have it, for this allots the reader too much power, and not merely receiving a text's meaning, for this elides the real effect that our intentionality has on the event that reading a work becomes. The events of reading made possible when one person picks up one book are utterly unique to those two, that person and that book. But the possibility of imaginative variation reminds us how many possibilities lie in wait for a person with a book in his hands. The concept of imaginative variation can be further refined if we think about attention as such and how it works.

Two models of attention

Husserl and Heidegger mention two different images relating to attention that suggest two very different relationships to reading. Husserl writes that "every present moment of experience has about it a fringe of experiences."[6] This fringe includes the background of experiences that a moment offers us but that we do not focus on. Turning toward the sea, for example, I see a bird plunge down for a fish. A boat may be floating in the background. The sea itself will offer movement and color for me to notice, but in this case, the bird has drawn my attention. The fringe of our attention also contains the moment just preceding the now, which inevitably colors the intentionality with which we approach the present moment. If my thoughts were dull and melancholy when I sensed the course of the bird's flight suddenly change, then his movement might be a refreshing awakening. The moment of his plunge is fringed on the opposite side by the moment that will follow it. If I walk off the side of a curb while watching him, then his catching his dinner will disappear in a tide of embarrassment. If I manage to keep walking undeterred, the sight is more likely to become secured in my mind through subsequent reflection. Altogether, Husserl observes that "no concrete experience can pass as independent in the

[6] Husserl, *Ideas*, 168.

full sense of the term. Each 'stands in need of completion' in respect of some connected whole, which in form and in kind is not something we are free to choose, but are rather bound to accept."[7] The image of the fringe of attention as Husserl describes it already carries the suggestion of reflective distance. It suggests a watcher at the side of a clearing, looking in, focused on something in the clearing but aware of the forest surrounding. Behind him is the moment he has just passed through, still influencing the mind. He turns toward the clearing before him, but he has not entered the clearing.

In "What is Called Thinking?" Heidegger suggests another image. He is talking about being interested and the etymological implications of the word versus the way that he feels people use it in 1951:

> Interest, *interesse*, means to be among and in the midst of things, or to be at the center of a thing and stay with it. But today's interest accepts as valid only what is interesting. And interesting is the sort of thing that can freely be regarded as indifferent the next moment and be replaced by something else, which then concerns us just as little as what went before.[8]

To be really interested in something, he suggests, really attending to it, we must let ourselves be pulled along by it. "Today's interest," he contends, lays responsibility for interest too much on the thing being attended to. He wants the interested person, instead, to commit to the chase, to commit to being interested. Always a little behind that which draws our attention, we will find ourselves surrounded by the absence of where it has been. "What withdraws from us, draws us along."[9] Heidegger's image is more like being in the clearing. He keeps his teacher's sense of movement and temporality, but one senses that the thinker, for Heidegger, is much more exposed somehow. The attention of an animal in a clearing differs very much from the attention of someone watching that animal.

Both of these kinds of attention are relevant for considering love and reading. Sometimes a book draws us into the absences it creates in much the manner that Heidegger describes. The most obvious example of this is

---

[7] Husserl, *Ideas*, 169.

[8] Martin Heidegger, "What is Called Thinking?," trans. J. Glenn Gray (New York: Perennial, 1976), 5.

[9] Heidegger, "What is Called Thinking?" 9.

suspense in novels. In William Godwin's *Caleb Williams*, the titular character has discovered his master's secret, that he had committed a murder and let another man and his son hang for it. Rather than allow this secret to get out, Squire Falkland, Caleb's employer, seizes control over Caleb by framing him for theft. Caleb is jailed, escapes, gets beaten by a gang of robbers, escapes again, is hosted by the same gang of robbers until one turns against him and he must escape again. Then on the road disguised as a beggar he overhears some laborers discussing his own story. "I was surprised, and not a little startled," the protagonist and narrator reflects, "to find them fall almost immediately into conversation about my history, whom with a slight variation of circumstances, they styled the notorious housebreaker, Kit Williams." Soon their conversation turns to the lucrative reward for capturing "Kit Williams," and Caleb must decide whether his beggar's disguise will be sufficient for him to remain in the pub with them or if he should try to run.[10] The story has trained the reader by this point to expect the worst for Caleb, so the suspense of the moment exercises power over most readers' attention. Godwin's younger contemporary William Hazlitt declared that "no one ever began *Caleb Williams* that did not read it through."[11] The prevailing structure of escape/pursuit/capture unites readers' emotional entanglement with Caleb and our hope that his innocence will triumph takes control of our attention.[12] Since knowledge about whether Caleb will be recognized or not is absent, the search for that information dominates our attitude.

In Elie Wiesel's *Night*, suspense and the weight of real individual lives lost both create the vacuum readers are drawn into. Gypsies are driving Wiesel and his fellow prisoners to another concentration camp across the countryside on a fresh spring day. In the passage below, the author's allusions to spring create hope, but not for long.

> The gypsies stopped near another barracks. They were replaced by SS, who surrounded us. Revolvers, machine guns, police dogs. The march had lasted

[10] William Godwin, *Things as They Are, or The Adventures of Caleb Williams*, ed. Maurice Hindle (London: Penguin, 1988), 244–245.

[11] William Hazlitt, *The Spirit of the Age, or Contemporary Portraits* (London: Colburn, 1825), 49–50.

[12] For a more thorough summary of the operation of suspense, see Geir Farner, *Literary Fiction: The Ways We Read Narrative Literature* (New York: Bloomsbury, 2014), 273–286.

> half an hour. Looking around me, I noticed that the barbed wires were behind us. We had left camp.
>
> It was a beautiful April day, the fragrance of spring was in the air. The sun was setting in the west.
>
> But we had been marching only a few moments when we saw the barbed wire of another camp. An iron door with this inscription over it: Work is Liberty!—Auschwitz.[13]

The prose withholds emotion. Using short clauses and simple words, it makes space for the narrative voice to receive whatever beauty or horror the day will offer. And then the name of the camp drops ungrammatically into the end of the last sentence like a spark drops into tinder.

In these cases, a work of literature exerts itself so forcibly on our attention that unless we have through habit or decision become resistant readers, we tend not to reflect on what is being offered to our attention. We tend not to choose what to be interested in, but to let the interest of the novel surround us and draw us forward. We are in the clearing, on the chase to return to the image suggested earlier. In that position as a reader, our attention is heightened. Not only does the book command the attention that other parts of our lives might be calling for (a phone ringing, a house that must be cleaned, the stop on the train we should be listening for), it also demands that we remain alert for details in the reading that we might pass over in a less attuned state. Is there a door that Caleb Williams can sneak out of? Is one of the laborers watching him? Is there going to be another sorting of people into fit and unfit when Wiesel reaches the camp? To what extent does the young narrator anticipate what Auschwitz will be?

These experiences of heightened attention in reading correspond to moments of heightened attention in our lives as lovers. Sometimes we are startled to attention by the need to protect a beloved, for example. The hope of a loving look returned, the fear of being turned away operate on us through the same mechanisms of attention activated in reading. Marion characterizes the physical play of two lovers as a radical passivity in which the lover becomes him or herself by receiving the gift of the awareness of his or her own flesh

---

[13] Elie Wiesel, *Night* (New York: Bantam Books, 2000), 37.

from the beloved. Such expectation commands the lover's full attention (*EP* 121). The magnitude of love calls for this undivided attention all the time.

> Love, coming from out there and going to infinity, can only come upon me if I renounce possessing it and hold myself strictly to the radicalized erotic reduction. Love thus only becomes thinkable according to the mode of the hoped for, of that which can only come upon me as the radically unseen and unwarranted. As such—as that which I can neither possess, nor provoke, nor merit, it will remain the unconditioned, and thus that which, on this condition, can give itself infinitely. Hope thus hopes for everything … It assists possibility. (*EP* 89)

Love demands that we attend fully to the beloved in hope without allowing expectations to shape that hope in a way that would prevent love from being fully revealed. But in reality, there are moments when situations bring forth this attention quite effortlessly, whereas in other moments lovers struggle to attend to the other at all.

In order for attention to "assist possibility" by allowing love to reveal itself without condition, it must go beyond the "blind intuition" (*EP* 96) of hoping for love in the abstract, and direct itself toward the object of our attention, which as Heidegger pointed out is withdrawing before us. Our attention is shaped by and shapes the person or book toward which it is directed. But however strongly our attention is determined by that at which it aims, the otherness of the text remains. Like the otherness of a person, the otherness of a text enables the attention we give it by creating the distance that desire traverses. With a novel like *Caleb Williams* or an autobiography like *Night*, we sense all that we want and cannot have withdrawing from us and drawing our desire. The reader wants to know that Caleb will be safe, but recognizes that the suspense that arises from not knowing is itself pleasurable. If we could somehow forget the distance between ourselves and Caleb and feel that we were being pursued ourselves, then the attention given to his dangerous situation would still be very much heightened but would lose its pleasure. But this never happens. Full identification always eludes the reader as it eludes the lover.

It would be disingenuous to pretend that all readings of great literature control the attention of every reader, or even that the same work of literature will exert this effect over the same reader every time she reads it. Rather than valorize a reading experience in which one's attention is forcibly manipulated by the text, it is better to accurately describe the means and measures of a text's controlling our attention and to articulate how developing a capacity for attention through reading can expand our capacity to enter into the erotic reduction with real beloveds.[14] Similarly there is no need to valorize the moment of being fully immersed in loving attention in person. Love calls sometimes for complete self-forgetfulness and a willingness to be drawn along by the beloved, but sometimes it calls for us to regard our beloved from the side of the clearing and reflect, still focusing on him or her in hope, but from more of a distance. An important question for the phenomenology of either love or reading is whether or not we can choose to give the heightened attention without a text or a beloved other demanding it from us. I think not. To claim that the extent of our attention given to a book or person is entirely under our control would be to deny the dependence on other consciousnesses that the erotic phenomenon underscores. We receive ourselves from our beloveds. Our reading experiences become part of the temporally unfolding process that we call our selves. The fact that there is not a "self" extricable from these processes prior to reading implies that our attention, too, expresses itself as shaped by other consciousnesses from the beginning.

Certainly readers can choose to read more or less carefully. They can give more attention to a single line or word than the structure of the text seems to invite if that line or world opens a line of inquiry he wants to pursue, but this kind of attention to a text imposes conditions. It does not "hope for everything" as love does in Marion's formulation, but hopes for just this one thing—a resonance within a text's historical discourse or a metrical innovation. Such conditional hope gives rise to conditional attention. It moves the reader to the top position in a hierarchical relationship to a text. If we see the habits of reading as effecting habits of love, then the regular exertion of dominance over a text will contribute to habits of objectifying and dominating the other. However, the implication that this seems to hold for reading—that a reader

---

[14] "Capacity" and "capability" should both be understood within the framework of the self's continual evolving in relation to others through love, not as a strength that an individual arrives at alone, as is usually suggested by the word "bildung."

should not willfully subject a text to a particular sort of attention that the text itself has not invited—needs to be dealt with more subtly.

The habit of giving conditional attention to a text will eventually erode a reader's capacity to attend unconditionally to a text, but that does not necessarily mean that the reading produced by conditional attention will not accrue more attention to a text in the long run. Cleanth Brooks's highly conditioned attention to "Ode on a Grecian Urn" comes to mind. By zeroing in on the text's ambiguities and technical proficiency, Brooks increases his readers' ability to receive these gifts from the text. He adds to the experience from which a reader can imaginatively draw. Jack Stillinger's "Fifty-nine Ways of Reading 'Ode on a Grecian Urn,'" written toward the end of a long career of teaching the poem, testifies to Brooks's contribution in opening up the poem for other readers. Stillinger enacts a rich performance of imaginative variation in his discussion of how the poem has been taught and can be read. His essay exemplifies the process by which one critic's limited and conditional attention can enable the hopeful, unconditional, well-experienced reading of another.

Pure and impure attention

In Marion's work, attention is often formulated in negative terms. He admonishes readers to pay attention *without* the imposition of categories of meaning that could limit what a phenomenon offers us. He advises viewers *not* to let a painting reach us only as a mirror of our own desire. Marion idealizes attention that is cleansed of structures that threaten to turn the phenomenon of encountering a work of art or a person into an instance in an argument or a mere fulfillment of our hopes. His contention is that phenomena themselves arrive as pure gift.[15] These gifts can only be received by "pure phenomenological consciousness."[16] While keeping this as an ideal, I would like to challenge this formulation as a practice and suggest that in love and in reading conditional attention can open possibilities for new kinds of attention to be paid to a work or person if readers and lovers are conceived as existing in a community. In a

---

[15] Marion, *Being Given*, 91.
[16] Marion, *Being Given*, 102.

community, a reader engages other readings as well as the reading of a primary text. Do these other readings—including critical articles, conversations, lectures—not also demand attention and also accrue to the individual reader's evolving personhood? As "utterly new" as phenomena are when we read a book or speak with a loved one, we never actually receive them as such. We interpret them from within our own horizon of experiences, from within the matrix of language itself, and from within communities of other readers.

The pure attention that a reader could pay a text as given—purely receptive with no categories constricting the text's arrival, purely devoted to love—can be theorized but never achieved. While Marion posits such moments of pure receptivity between two lovers in the flesh or in a moment of spiritual revelation, such pure receptivity would fail to receive a written work. Language cannot function without the meaning of words being restricted. If a word could mean anything, it would mean nothing. This is why, when Marion seeks a way to describe a lover's purest speech, he writes, "I say nothing about nothing, but I address myself desperately to the other" (*EP* 145). The attention we give to works of literature then, is inevitably conditional, impure. That does not mean that readers cannot aspire to more pure attention, however, and it does not leave conditional attention without value.

Moreover, there is more than one kind of negatively defined attention, and not all of them are equally loving. In *The Second Sex*, Simone de Beauvoir famously critiques the "myth of a woman" that can be used for the subjugation of women. She argues that by viewing women as mysterious, men can excuse themselves from attending to an individual woman's unique and surprising combination of tendencies and whims. Although de Beauvoir implies that there is no comparably damaging "myth of man," the concept of authentic relationality that she tries to develop through her critique of the myth of woman does not depend on a gender-specific focus. "The subjective game" of idolizing the mysteriousness of the beloved can, she explains, "go all the way from vice to mystical ecstasy" and can be played by any gender. This game can excuse flattering someone into a sexual romp on the one hand and justifying a kind of content-less idealization of the beloved on the other. For many this game is "a more attractive experience than an authentic relation with a human being" because it is easier and remains more fully within the control of the ego.[17] Luxuriating in the mystery of the beloved other resembles Marion's negative preparation for receiving saturated phenomena, be they book or person, in that accepting mystery eliminates categories of understanding that might confine the givenness that a book or another person offers. In Marion's ideal of pure attention, we attend to the phenomenon as given, but focusing on the elimination of categorical restrictions can lead our attention away from the given and toward mystery as a possibility or our own attentive faculties. Idealizing the unknowability of the other can obscure what he or she gives as easily as any conceptual category. Similarly, idealizing the unknowability of a text could obscure it. Rather than opening a reading, the conviction that a text must come to us with no preconceptions could blind readers to the preconceptions that we all inevitably do have. In order to explore the ways these preconceptions shape the attention of even the most open readers, I turn now to Gadamer.

Gadamer uses the term "prejudice" to describe the concepts that shape attention. He shakes the term free of its negative connotations and uses it to mean simply "a judgment that is rendered before all the elements that determine a situation have been finally examined" (283). Prejudices both precede every reading and arise during the course of that reading. They enable understanding and facilitate pleasure. It is readers' prejudicial association of spring and the promise of new life that allows Elie Wiesel to make the discovery that he has moved to Auschwitz so appropriately devastating. Gadamer points out that the hermeneutic circle operates by the text creating and adjusting readers' prejudices along the way. He concerns himself more, however, with the prejudices that readers bring to a book. He celebrates literature's ability to expose prejudices, not so that they can be dispelled in every case, but so that they can be brought to light. A "hermeneutically trained consciousness" learns to be "sensitive to the text's alterity" by recognizing the prejudices called into operation by an act of reading.[18] Gadamer distinguishes between prejudices that are "due to human authority" and those "due to overhastiness" and argues that those due to human authority need not be discarded automatically. They

---

[17] Simone de Beauvoir, *The Second Sex*, trans. Constance Borde and Sheila Malovany-Chevallier (New York: Vintage, 2011), 269.
[18] Gadamer, *Truth and Method*, 282.

are mediated by reason and tradition. We decide, using reason, whether or not to accept the authority through which prejudice-begetting beliefs reach us. If such prejudices reach us through tradition, we similarly can use reason to accept or discard them.[19]

Tradition commands readerly attention to texts in several obvious ways. It helps determine the amount of attention readers feel they should pay to formal innovation. Critics reading Wordsworth's *The Prelude*, for example, attend to the overall structure, the evolving image, the choice of word. They find innovation in his portrayal of memory, his use of dreams, the language of sound, and the sound of language. All these innovations are there to be found. But readers have not looked for them in Christopher Thomson's *The Autobiography of an Artisan*, an autobiography contemporary with Wordsworth's.[20] Thomson trained to become a shipwright, but excelled at drawing and painting. He traveled as a scene-painter and actor for several years and finally settled down as a house-painter. His autobiography challenges the association between occupational success and personal fulfillment that the title leads readers to expect. He posits a communally-oriented self and invites the reader to feel herself a part of his community through the manipulation of second-person address. His autobiography is innovative and describes artisanal life during a crucial historical moment. However, it does not reach most readers as part of the tradition of nineteenth-century autobiography, so tradition does not lead them to attend to innovations in the work of an unknown house-painter.

In addition to determining how closely readers attend to a text, tradition also helps determine the way readers prioritize aspects of an individual text. In this way, tradition relates to the community-embeddedness of reading mentioned earlier. Stillinger's "Fifty-Nine Ways of Looking at 'Ode on a Grecian Urn'" bears the mark of the traditions that Stillinger was trained in and the tradition that he and his students evolved through years of reading in community together. Critical traditions include so-called schools of critical

---

[19] Gadamer, *Truth and Method*, 284–296.
[20] Christopher Thomson, *The Autobiography of an Artisan* (London: Chapman, 1847). See also Cassandra Falke, *Literature by the Working Class: English Autobiography, 1820–1848* (Amherst: Cambria, 2013).

practice, but also institutional practices that more easily go unnoticed such as the use of anthologies or the footnoting of obscure allusions. These traditions nevertheless alter readers' future prejudices, unless individual readers evoke reasons to dispel them.

Perhaps the most pervasive of these traditions, the category that most often prevents texts from giving themselves to us fully, is the aesthetic disposition itself, which leads readers to evaluate literature, post-Kant, from a position of disinterest. Disinterested reading, as a categorical form of attention to a text, has preserved its position of privilege, not because it is always rigorous, but because of its lingering association with class privilege. Jacques Rancière has gracefully made the point that aesthetic experience has to a large extent been freed from the exclusionary practices of education and ownership that kept the professional experience of art and literature artificially separated from diverse non-professional experiences of them. He writes that "works of art are no longer determined by their destination as illustrations of faith or power" and that "they are no longer appreciated according to rules of taste defined by a specific public." This historical shift "contributes to the reframing of the common landscape, to the reframing of the distribution of the possible" in thinking about art and literature.[21]

Disinterested reading has rightly been critiqued as an impossibility and a politically debilitating ideal. At an even more primary level, however, the question of disinterest is problematic for a phenomenology of literature since phenomenology takes interest in structuring the reception of every phenomenon. It is attention born of interest that phenomenalizes art at all. In valuing interest, phenomenology offers a means of rejoining reading practices traditionally valued by the academy with practices traditionally dismissed as personal—reading for escapism, for comfort, for inspiration, or to articulate desire. These reading practices are profoundly interested. These manners of attending to a literary work need not threaten to overtake or dilute more rigorously developed forms of attention that claim precedence in the academy, but blocking them out entirely delimits readers' ability to accept texts' invitations to attend to them fully.

---

[21] Jacques Rancière, "A Few Remarks on the Method of Jacques Rancière," *Parallax* 15, no. 3 (2009): 122.

Some practices of intentional reading look highly dubious within the institutional setting of the academy—reading with attention shaped by nationalism, class aspiration, the fondness for someone who was fond of that book, the echo of home, the sense of support during a crisis in our lives. But an approach to reading that dismisses these forms of personal interest out of hand unnecessarily restricts the power literature can have. I once taught a student named Pamela. Pamela was a guard at a prison in Port Arthur, Texas, and she was stabbed in the lungs by a prisoner there. She was in college retraining for a possible new career while she healed. One day while covering scansion, I quoted the first lines of "Invictus," a Victorian poem by William Ernest Henley. Pamela took it up after the first two lines, shyly and self-mockingly at first and then with more confidence. She recited all three verses to an astounded class of tired, night-school students. As was the case with a lot of my students there, Pamela had been raised by a single mother who woke early to fit two shifts and two different jobs into each day. Pamela's mother had the poem by her bed to help her get up in the morning. I cannot think of a good reason to exclude Pamela's kind of appreciation for that poem from a serious discussion of literature's power with regard to the politics of labor, gender, ethnicity, or phenomenology, but conversely, I cannot think of many critical theoretical practices that include it.

Admiration and contemplation

I would like to conclude by discussing two overlooked mental acts that readers perform when they give attention to a book. Each of these acts opens new opportunities for love in person and for charitable reading. Neither is new, but I think their value as critical acts has been whittled away during the decades in which literary theory has focused on what readers can do to a work of literature rather than what a work of literature can do to (or give to) its readers. The two acts are admiration and contemplation. The first, admiration, refers to a process we perform before a reading. Marion defines admiration as "the most powerful exercise possible of the look" and praises Descartes' definition: "Admiration is an unexpected surprise of the soul, making the latter consider with attention the objects that seem to it rare and extraordinary."[22] Admiration prepares the way for attentive reading, readying us for the plot, the word, the image that will surprise us. The reader who opens a book prepared to admire it disciplines the prejudices that he perceives himself to create in the process of reading, so that those judgments that threaten to impede a work's ability to give itself are held in check. Some books may surprise the soul with such force that even an unprepared reader will be startled into admiration, but how many smaller wonders are missed by readers who are not prepared to be surprised? A prejudicial judgment that a plot will be predictable or dialogue stilted conditions the reading of the rest of the book from the moment it is made.

The second mental act comes after reading. This is the act of contemplation. Husserl privileged contemplation as a practice of attending to our own life-world, the world that we are inside of but rarely see: "Contemplation is privileged to the extent that it reveals the structures of the world and has them as theme."[23] As a reader finishes reading a powerful book, the world of the book merges with the structures of the world we look out on. A book may explicitly thematize some element of a reader's life-world. Perhaps one thinks about idealizing a lover after reading *The Great Gatsby*. A reader can also bring attention to an element of the book's world through contemplation, explicitly thematizing the questions that a book implicitly asks and bringing extratextual experience into that process of thematization. I can ask, in light of *The Great Gatsby's* last line what it means that we "beat on, boats against the current, borne back ceaselessly into the past."[24] I will never know. As an imaginative figure at the end of beautiful novel, the picture of myself as a boat is not reducible to a concept. Even without the context of the novel, the line gives itself as a saturated phenomenon, exceeding whatever intentionality I could deploy to anticipate it or try to pin it down. Even when I see the white facing page, signaling the end of the novel and I know that the line is coming, it exceeds the concept left by my prior experiences of the line as long as I allow it to. But contemplation does not have to pin it down.

[22] Descartes, quoted in Marion, *In Excess*, 59.
[23] Edmund Husserl, *Experience and Judgement*, trans. James Spencer Churchill and Karl Ameriks (Evanston: Northwestern University Press, 1973), 65.
[24] Fitzgerald, *The Great Gatsby*, 192.

Contemplation can use the work of literature to perform imaginative variation on the world in the same way that it can use what the world has given us before we sit down to read to perform imaginative variation on the text. Think of the line as a series of notes. I can play them over and over in other contexts and with other emphases. Charles Suhor describes contemplative reading as a practice that is "neither doctrinal, nor analytical, a perspective that even goes beyond aesthetic experience in the usual sense of the term."[25] Contemplation is speculative, rather than practical; exploratory, rather than teleological. In relation to reading, contemplation allows readers to discover how their horizons have been changed in the process of reading if they thematize the process of reading itself as the object of contemplation. The structures of argument, which are so advantageous in the elaboration of a critical interpretation, constrain the arrival of insights about the relation between an event of reading and the rest of our life because they predetermine what insights we will accept. The less-constrained processes of contemplation and admiration act as important compliments to the traditions of argument that dominate the professional reading of literature.

The act of contemplative reading presumes that a reader will see the ideas of a text as relevant for understanding the world, but a book's potential for meaning need not presume predicative content. In Marion's concise phrase, "Dialogue is more invocation than predication."[26] He differentiates between predicative language used by science to refer to things in predictable, repetitive, and therefore reliable ways and the language of invocation through which an event of saturated phenomenality, including the appearance of another person, can be accomplished. This distinction cannot be maintained ontologically. It would be possible for the same sentence to occur in a scientific journal, a novel, or a conversation at dinner. But it accords with the idea that the receiver of a gift enables that gift's appearing, "for what gives shows itself only as much as it is received by the gifted."[27]

---

[25] Charles Suhor, "Contemplative Reading—The Experience, the Idea, the Applications," *The English Journal* 91, no. 4 (March 2002).

[26] Jean-Luc Marion, personal interview (March 28, 2015).

[27] Marion, *Being Given*, 310.

A critic reading within the erotic reduction will try to receive a text as both invocative and predicative. A critic can read a text, charitably, as though it were spoken to her precisely. Welcoming a text as intended for me personally does not limit the hermeneutic potential of the text because I am not a fixed and bounded object. I am unfolding still and will do so in relation to what I read. Receiving a text as intended for me does connect what the text offers to the rest of my life because the text is no longer separable from me. It has become part of my experience. Conversely, a text does remain separable from me, free and approachable by anyone through understanding. To some extent, a critic must approach the language of a text as predication, referring to practices, events, ways of being and objects that I understand through experience of similar phenomena because the critical account of reading I produce will need to communicate by means of both predicative and invocative language. Certainly I will use predicative language, scientific language as Marion says, in my writing about a text, because I will refer to formal features of the text itself. These two modes of receiving a text—as communicated to me or as predicative—alternate in most critical practice, but the distinction allows for the value of each to be recognized.

It is through the reception of a text as communication that literature assists us in maintaining a phenomenological view of the world itself. In a wonderful passage that anticipates Husserl's exploration of the reduction by 150 years, Johann Gottfried Herder says that:

> Every inherited concept deadens a nerve by which the soul might have discovered it for itself … [H]ow effortlessly … we assume the outcome of a lengthy operation of the human mind, without ourselves running through the operation that originally produced it.

This inheritance, he laments, "benumbs our power to understand the concept as inwardly as if we had discovered it by ourselves."[28] The phenomenological reduction is an attempt to reanimate the soul and experience things for themselves. The attention we pay to literature becomes the attention we can

---

[28] Johann Gottfried Herder, *Selected Writings on Aesthetics*, trans. Gregory Moore (Princeton: Princeton University Press, 2006), 213.

give the world because it expands the aperture through which we receive the world we share with others. The self-forgetfulness that reading makes possible enables the contemplation that brings forth connections between reading and the rest of our lives. And both self-forgetfulness and contemplation help us to attend to our beloveds.

6

Being Overwhelmed

One of Marion's most significant contributions to phenomenology is his concept of the saturated phenomenon. The saturated phenomenon provides the framework for Marion's understanding of events as common as a train journey or as rare and wonderful as the birth of a child.[1] In every instance, saturated phenomena by definition exceed our ability to perceive them. As mentioned, saturated phenomena are those in which the intuition offered us exceeds the intention that we turn toward the phenomenon. Since under the erotic reduction, we do not preexist the appearing of a saturated phenomenon as stable subjectivities, saturated phenomena also *extend* our ability to perceive them. Marion reasserts time and time again that the ego does not precede phenomenality but is in fact constructed by means of it, so every book we read contributes to our evolving selfhood. The concept of saturated phenomena is important for an inquiry into love and reading because it provides the basic elements through which both love and reading can be described.

While saturated phenomena may be astounding, they are not rare. Marion gives as one example of a saturated phenomena a lecture.[2] That lecture, he says was an "absolutely unique, irreproducible, and largely unpredictable event."[3] Consequently, it was and will forever be inaccessible to intention. The listeners had no precise precedent that would have allowed them to intend it beforehand, and none could later intend through memory exactly what had taken place.

---

[1] Marion, *In Excess*, 41–43. Marion calls birth "the event *par excellence*," because "it *gives me to myself* when it gives itself." Emphasis in original.

[2] Jean-Luc Marion, "The Event, the Phenomenon and the Revealed," in *Transcendence in Philosophy and Religion*, ed. James E. Faulconer (Bloomington: Indiana University Press, 2003), 88–90.

[3] Marion, "The Event, the Phenomenon and the Revealed," 89.

Because of the limitedness of our intentionality, our lives unfold as a series of these saturated phenomena as our encounters with seemingly stable objects take place in ways that we cannot predict, capture, or fully remember.[4] In the words of Walter Pater, "Every moment some form grows perfect in hand or face; some tone on the hills or the sea is choicer than the rest," and we miss it.[5] Terry Eagleton critiques phenomenological criticism as "naively avant-garde" if it implies that "everyday experience is bankrupt." He mocks the idea that discourse becomes valuable "only by being ruptured, thickened, dislocated, condensed, heightened or pared to a vanishing point."[6] Marion's phenomenology of love risks the opposite extreme. He describes everyday life as unrecountably rich, so rich that one wonders how the experience of art could prove its value in competing with the rest of life for the adonne's attention. But instead of picturing art and daily events as competing with each other, Marion's phenomenology asserts art's ability to reawaken us to the brilliance of life's everyday offerings.

According to Marion, we encounter saturated phenomena in an event, a painting, the face of another, or the flesh. These four categories of phenomena correspond to Kant's four categories of understanding—quantity, quality, modality, and relation. Kant calls these "ontological predicates," which is to say that, by being in place, these categories allow us to make judgments about what things are and how they compare to other things or themselves at other times.[7] Kant had originally formulated these categories to describe the limits of our perceptive abilities, but for Marion, the recognition of these limits facilitates the recognition of all the moments when life exceeds these limits. Marion's description of saturated phenomenality resembles Kant's description of the sublime in some important ways, especially in the ways that both philosophers describe the first stage of aesthetic experience.[8] In a famous passage from his *Critique of Judgment*, Kant describes sublimity as an experience—an event—rather than a property of objects found in nature:

---

[4] Marion, *In Excess*, 33.
[5] Walter Pater, *Studies in the History of the Renaissance* (Oxford: Oxford University Press, 2010), 119.
[6] Terry Eagleton, *The Event of Literature* (Yale: Yale University Press, 2013), 92–93.
[7] Immanuel Kant, *Critique of the Power of Judgment*, trans. James Meredith, and ed. Nicolas Walker (Oxford: Oxford University Press, 2007), 68.
[8] For Marion's discussion of Kantian sublimity, which he considers monstrous but theologically fertile, see "The Saturated Phenomenon," in *Philosophy and the Theological Turn: The French Debate*, 214.

For the sublime, in the strict sense of the word, cannot be contained in any sensuous form, but rather concerns ideas of reason, which, although no adequate presentation of them is possible, may be excited and called into the mind by that very inadequacy itself which does admit of sensuous presentation. Thus the broad ocean agitated by storms cannot be called sublime. Its aspect is horrible, and one must have stored one's mind in advance with a rich stock of ideas, if such an intuition is to raise it to the pitch of a feeling which is itself sublime—sublime because the mind has been incited to abandon sensibility and employ itself upon ideas involving higher finality.[9]

Kant here suggests that the experience of the sublime is the experience of the mind's inadequacy, as much as an experience of a storm on the ocean or some other overwhelming event. He stresses that it is the limitation of our mental categories, our "rich stock of ideas" that prevents us from receiving all that the ocean has to give us, but also that without this limitedness, we would not recognize the that the stormy ocean *is* giving us more than what we receive. The mis-fit he describes between what someone looking seaward can accept and what the stormy ocean can give resembles Marion's articulation of saturated phenomenality very much. Using the language of phenomenology, Marion does not examine concepts or ideas as though they were separable from experience and stably placed in the mind, but he would agree with Kant that previous experiences shape our perception of saturated phenomenality in the present.

The important difference between Kantian sublimity and Marionian saturation is what each philosopher presumes happens after an overwhelming experience has passed. For Kant, the viewer uses his or her reason to generate a conception of the sublime experience that exceeds the experience itself. At the base of a 14,000 foot mountain, for example, I will be offered the sublime experience of viewing something much larger than my field of vision. Kant suggests that my previous experience with mountains will combine with my reason to facilitate my conception of the entire mountain, even though I could never aesthetically experience the entire mountain at one time.[10] It would not

---

[9] Kant, *Critique of Judgement*, 76.
[10] Kant, *Critique of Judgment*, 79.

be necessary that I know beforehand how many feet this specific mountain is or how it rates in terms of climbing difficulty, only that I have seen mountains before. Once I know that I can conceive of the whole mountain using reason, the sublime experience "determines the mind to regard the elevation of nature beyond our reach as equivalent to a presentation of ideas."[11] This very Kantian moment wherein I reasonably conceptualize more mountain than I can see gives me the satisfaction that my capacity for ideation exceeds my aesthetic capacity. In Kant's words, "we may become conscious of our superiority over nature within, and thus also over nature without us (as exerting influence upon us)."[12] For Kant, the initial discomfort caused by a viewer's perceptive inadequacy is replaced by a more comfortable second stage in which the viewer realizes she is capable of understanding her own lack of understanding. Metacognitive reflection thereby reestablishes the viewer's sense that she is adequate to the world in which she finds herself.

Marion, in contrast, neither recognizes nor aims for the superiority of a viewer over nature, be it "within" or "without us." He accepts perceptive inadequacy as part of the human condition and renders it positive. Our perception is inadequate because the gift of the world is so great. Marion considers "phenomena where the duality between intention (signification) and intuition (fulfillment) certainly remains," but where "an intuitive givenness ... must be allowed to overflow" any conception that I could bring to bear on it.[13] For Marion, there is no after-the-fact metacognition that can encompass either the event of saturated phenomenality or the event of my perceiving my aesthetic incapacity through reason. This would require a third event (the viewing of the mountain being the first, and my measuring it by means of reason rather than sense being the second) in which what I perceive is not the mountain itself but my own ability to conceive of but not see it. Marion never forbids after-the-fact recollections of saturated phenomena. I may reflect again and again on one amazing view of one amazing mountain. But, such a recollection will always be another event, the event of recollection temporally divided forever from the

---

[11] Kant, *Critique of Judgment*, 98.
[12] Kant, *Critique of Judgement*, 94.
[13] Marion, *In Excess*, 112.

seeing of a mountain. This third event will never overtake in a timeless mental space the original moment of being overwhelmed.

The discomfort of a viewer facing his or her own incapacity to take in an experience becomes a part of that person's evolving selfhood. It is never cancelled out by a succeeding moment of comfort derived from a recognition of metacognitive power. This is for two reasons. First, Marion conceives of the self as grounded in givenness in general and love in particular. The self is thus "relieved of its royal transcendental status" and "no longer precedes the phenomenon.... [I]t is received from what it receives"[14] The mountain becomes part of my self without being at all subjected to it when I experience its overwhelming phenomenality because there was no transcendental self there to begin with. Secondly, recognizing the mountain's presentation to me as an event rather than an object, Marion does not allow for the possibility that it could ever be adequately anticipated or received by anyone, no matter what her capacity of reason.

How does the saturated phenomenality of a mountain or saturated phenomenality as such relate to reading? In the discussion of Marion's four kinds of saturated phenomena below, I argue that reading reaches us through three of the four categories. We experience reading as an event, the book reaches us (like other art forms) inevitably as an idol, and it can reach us as an icon. The fact that literature can never reach us through Marion's fourth category of saturated phenomenality—the flesh—is also significant. Each of these categories is explained in more depth below. The more general significance of Marion's saturated phenomenality to reading is the relationship between the concept and hermeneutics. Marion writes, "I cannot assign a single meaning to the immensity of lived experiences that happen to me." This applies equally to mountains and works of literature, and this is precisely what Kant would have had us do, master the mountain as concept. To regard the mountain is to fit it within us. Instead, Marion says, "I can only pursue [lived experiences] by unceasingly multiplied and modified significations, in a hermeneutic without end."[15] Every view of a mountain gives rise to innumerable subsequent hermeneutical events.

[14] Marion, *In Excess*, 50.
[15] Marion, *In Excess*, 112–113.

Some critics have worried that Marion's saturated phenomenality implies an impossibility of interpreting events, but he implies quite the opposite, "a hermeneutic without end." The use of the singular "a hermeneutic" here implies that the interpretation of a lived experience carries forward the insufficiently captured first experience of book or mountain as well as all of our prior attempts to recall or interpret that first experience. A critical act includes the residue of our first encounter with a book (itself actually a multifarious experience that usually takes place across multiple days and moods) as well as the residue of all or our subsequent acts of reading, recollection, or interpretation. The endless hermeneutic includes all of these in the experience of picking up a book again to write about it, tell a friend about it or read it again. Each of these activities will activate that endless hermeneutic differently, but at the point when we begin any one of them, the hermeneutical act we begin is actually a continuation of a process that that same book has initiated before. Experience spills forward like a river with seams of prior directionality and force modifying the forward-moving whole. It is not stored away in epistemological categories like so many drawers in a chest.

The question of whether the book or the reader initiates that hermeneutical process is worth contemplating briefly before examining each of the kinds of saturated phenomena in detail. Marion recognizes a kind of hermeneutic circle that exceeds questions of aesthetic engagement and dominates lived experience generally. He recognizes that any reduction—to phenomenology, or being, givenness, cognition, or love—involves both the givenness of the reduction itself and a person's acceptance of it. Discussing the history of phenomenology, he writes with regard to every reduction that it is "neither a question of one concept among others nor of doctrine to discuss, but of an operation." Because a reduction claims to bring "back the semblance of the appearing to the full appearing of phenomena," it claims priority as an operation, but this operation implies an operator—a self, a reader. When a self enters into a reduction, it is both a performance of an act and something that that self steps into. Consequently, "this operator him- or herself is found modified—and essentially—by the reduction that he or she puts to work."[16]

[16] Marion, *In Excess*, 46.

The "operator" who sees a work of literature as gift, choosing to enter Marion's reduction to givenness, becomes more capable of recognizing and receiving the gifts reading offers. The operator who further enters the erotic reduction esteems books in reference to love. He or she does become more capable as a lover (or a hater) because this reduction operates on the operator herself, but this change in the operator is not needed to somehow justify the erotic reduction. To imply that it did would be to make the ego again the measure of phenomenality itself. I argue, with Marion, that the erotic reduction facilitates the full appearing of phenomena more than the reductions that were proposed before it. This is because all things, before they are things, are given as gifts constituted by means of love or hate. The lover chooses to enter the erotic reduction as an operator so that things will give themselves to him more fully. As with other reductions, he finds himself modified by it, but he never becomes the measure or the enabler of erotic givenness itself.

The erotic reduction operates prior to but also with the modes of saturation through which reading reaches us. These experiences will not become more interpretively rich, however, if we say flatly that an individual experience has a positive or negative valence because it does or does not make the self in question a better lover. Even if we preserve at base the commitment to love as the precondition of books, authors, readers, and reading ever appearing, then the manner of their appearing must still be considered in order to make possible hermeneutic processes that are not only endless, but also nuanced. The next section considers the four modes of appearing that Marion labels saturated phenomena and considers the hermeneutical possibilities for reading suggested by each of them. Since a work of literature can give itself through three of these modes, a reader can explore the interpretive possibilities of all of them in the act of imaginative variation.

Reading as event

The first of the four categories of saturated phenomena is the event, which is saturated according to quantity. Our intention proves inadequate for events because we cannot anticipate what will unfold, cannot recall all that has happened afterwards, and cannot take in everything that the event offers us as it happens. The description of the event comes first, because although Marion defines it as one among four modes of saturated phenomenality, event-ness characterizes all four modes. In fact, according to Marion, every object is actually the "simple illusion of an a-temporal event."[17] This includes common-law phenomena like the pen I pick up to write with as well as saturated phenomena like paintings. Common-law phenomenality and saturated phenomenality need not be considered two exclusive categories. They are rather two poles of experience. Reading occurs, at times, more like a common-law event when what a text offers me matches my expectations. Pulling up to a red, octagonal sign in the United States, I expect to read "Stop," and I find my expectations fulfilled. The event of reading a stop sign is therefore not saturated even though it is an event. It does not take long to realize, however, that even apparently simple events of reading unfold in ways that exceed our expectations. If I read a recipe for pound cake, I may anticipate some of the ingredients, but not the precise proportions. A very simple act of reading thus becomes somewhat saturated as an event because it involves surprise. But surprise is only a limited experience of saturated phenomenality. If reading a recipe fulfills the minimum qualifications for saturated phenomenality, it does not draw out the full richness of the concept. Saturated phenomenality suggests a whole spectrum of ways to acknowledge the vastness of the gift of experience in relation to what we take in. It is humbling and overwhelming, and recipes (usually) are neither of these things.

A literary text offers much greater complexity than a recipe, but for all that, may or may not reach readers as a more fully saturated phenomenon. Christina Gschwandtner identifies "degrees of givenness" in her 2014 book of that title, and this is a useful concept for considering the event of reading. The possibility of measuring, or even describing, degrees of saturation at first seems to contradict the idea of saturation itself since a quality of saturated phenomena is their ability to exceed all categorization, all measurement, and even all description. But even if we accept that a description must fail to adequately delineate the degrees of saturation of specific events that can

---

[17] Marion, *In Excess*, 38.

possibly occur, recognizing the forces that contribute to a phenomenon of reading reaching us as more-or-less saturated will add subtlety to our means of describing specific acts of reading. These forces seem to be fourfold: the degree of a work's complexity, the power of a work to make visible that which could not previously be seen, the reader's disposition toward the work, and the compatibility between a reader's preparation to receive a work and what the work gives.

All of these forces are to be conceived phenomenologically. They depend on the act of reading that a specific person, constituted in love, performs in a specific time, with a specific text. The complexity of the text, to take one of these concepts as an example, cannot be conceived as existing objectively in the text alone, prior to reading. Some texts may tend to give rise to more complex readings than others, but this has to do with perceptions of authorship, readerly expectations and the sense of history that characterize the relationship between reader and text as much as it has to do with specific rhyme patterns or subplots. If a reader expects a short lyric poem to be complex because William Carlos Williams wrote it, then the poem will unfold with greater complexity for that reader. His reading practice can then be passed on to other readers, but there will always be the reader for whom "The Red Wheelbarrow" remains a simple, imagistic poem.

Similarly, if a reader encounters "A Sick Rose" after agreeing to write an essay on Romantic period poetic form and meter, then the elegant reading that Susan Steward offers in "Romantic Meter and Form" becomes possible in a way that it would not have been if that critic had accepted a commission to write an essay on Blake's opposition to what he felt was the corruption of the state.[18] In a reading that privileges the sense of history over poetic form, the force of the poem will arise from the boldness of a lyric poem that takes on issues like child labor and war-fed capitalism in eight lines and a rosebud. Saturated phenomenality does not privilege one form of complexity over another. It does not even privilege complexity as such. Reading Marion, one feels that he sees

---

[18] Susan Stewart, "Romantic Meter and Form," *Cambridge Companion to British Romantic Poetry* (Cambridge: Cambridge University Press, 2008). An essay about Blake's critique of the state could recall an equally saturated event of reading the poem, but it would reflect the intentionality of that critic and that assignment.

abstract art forms as more admirably saturated that less abstract forms, but that, I would argue, is his expectation as a viewer/reader more than a property of saturated phenomenality. As a concept, saturated phenomenality does not prescribe aesthetic or moral value. Each of the four forces influencing a reader's reception of the saturated event of reading (degree of complexity, a work's rendering of visibility, the reader's disposition, and the compatibility between a reader's preparation to receive a work and what the work gives) can operate in relation to a range of priorities in reading, both those priorities that are acknowledged and those that are unseen.

Whether banal or extraordinary, events amaze us because of their unforeseeability, and reading events offer this. Take an apparently simple poem as an example. Dudley Randall describes a mother who forbids her child to march in a civil rights rally in Birmingham but instead dresses her in her best white gloves and shoes and sends her to church. The mother has clear expectations:

> The mother smiled to know her child
> Was in the sacred place,

The poem's tidy a-b-c-b rhyme scheme and child-friendly vocabulary does not prepare readers for the forceful volta, or change, in the next two stanzas, in spite of the frank language of "dogs" and "hoses" that the mother had earlier used to warn her girl away from the rally. Here is the poem in full:

> "Mother dear, may I go downtown
> Instead of out to play,
> And march the streets of Birmingham
> In a Freedom March today?"
>
> "No, baby, no, you may not go,
> For the dogs are fierce and wild,
> And clubs and hoses, guns and jails
> Aren't good for a little child."
>
> "But, mother, I won't be alone.
> Other children will go with me,

And march the streets of Birmingham
To make our country free."

"No, baby, no, you may not go,
For I fear those guns will fire.
But you may go to church instead
And sing in the children's choir."

She has combed and brushed her night-dark hair,
And bathed rose petal sweet,
And drawn white gloves on her small brown hands,
And white shoes on her feet.

The mother smiled to know her child
Was in the sacred place,
But that smile was the last smile
To come upon her face.

For when she heard the explosion,
Her eyes grew wet and wild.
She raced through the streets of Birmingham
Calling for her child.

She clawed through bits of glass and brick,
Then lifted out a shoe.
"O, here's the shoe my baby wore,
But, baby, where are you?"

"The Ballad of Birmingham" recalls the bombing of 16th Street Baptist Church in September of 1963, which killed three African-American girls while they were changing into their choir robes. The event overwhelmed not only the parents of the children and the local community, but also sent a message that the violent resistance to civil rights had reached truly terroristic proportions, realigning the nation's understanding of the lengths to which segregationists would go. An extreme event like this dramatically illustrates the saturation according to quantity. We struggle to find room for an event like this within us. Thinking about reading the poem as its own event, a whole range of degrees of saturation becomes possible. Randall originally published the poem as a broadside in 1965, when memory of the event was still fresh in public memory.[19] Nevertheless, not everyone was equally concerned with the fate of a Baptist Church in Alabama, so it is easy to imagine a reader encountering Randall's sharply printed second edition of his broadside in 1965 as the first news of the bombing. Opening the striking black cover of the card-printed broadside, a reader would find the poem's subtitle, "(On the Bombing of a Church in Birmingham, Alabama, 1963)," printed above the poem itself.

Broadsides had been used in the eighteenth and nineteenth centuries to sensationalize violent crimes and muster political support, and Randall's broadside serves both of these purposes amicably, but it would be a heartless reader who saw the poem as a political statement before registering the overwhelming human loss it portrays. This imagined innocent reader, for whom the poem is the first news about the bombing, would, if no bias stood in the way, experience the ballad as heavily saturated. The ballad form and lightness of the broadside would hardly seem able to contain it. Randall only allows the force of the event he describes to break the poem's rhythmic form at the most intense moments. The word "explosion" does not scan iambically; it hardly scans at all. "But that smile was the last smile" ends on an unaccented syllable with no emphatic following syllable to complete the line. The poem then returns, as the mother clearly must, to the forms established before the explosion interrupts the poem's form and the lives that the poem describes. Even a reader who would not care to describe the rhythmic features of the poem would find his encounter with the news of the bombing shaped by their influence.

If we imagine another reader, however—a student perhaps sitting three seats to the right of the back corner of the classroom looking surreptitiously at his hands under his desk while a teacher reads this poem—it is easy to imagine someone who encounters the poem as something very near to a common law phenomenon. He may not have anticipated the exact words of

---

[19] For more on Randall's broadsides and the Broadside Press, see Melba Joyce Boyd, *Wrestling with the Muse: Dudley Randall and the Broadside Press* (New York: Columbia University Press, 2003), Chapter 8.

the poem and will not bother to recall them, but he expected the teacher to say something rhym-y with what he perceives as only remote historical value for him. Between these extremes occur many possible variations. The question that the erotic reduction invites us to ask is, "How does our reception of the saturated event of reading relate to love?" The ideal lover hopes all things, to paraphrase Paul (1 Cor. 13:7). She approaches the beloved not only expecting to have her preconceptions overthrown, but looking forward to it, assuming that the discovery she makes in each new encounter with the beloved will reconfirm her unreasonable reasons for loving. No one achieves this ideal, and no beloved justifies this hope. Nevertheless, hope conditions the lover's ability to receive the event of the beloved's arrival (even conditions it in aspiring to unconditionality), and the arrival of the beloved provides that structure that allows us to understand receptive reading. Marion explains that love "only becomes thinkable according to the mode of the hoped for, of that which can only come upon me as the radically unseen and unwarranted."[20] This is because a lover denies all possession of the beloved in order to allow him to appear freely and without condition. Hope, which resists conditionality but creates a free space in which the intended can appear, also provides the mode through which a work of literature can appear most fully.

Recall the case of the imagined reader who had no prior knowledge of the Birmingham church bombing and experienced the appearing of that event at the same time as experiencing the event of Randall's poem. In this case, the combined surprise of these two events startled this reader into receptivity. Even if he had not tried to make himself receptive to the event of reading, the poem arrested his attention and he became receptive. Sometimes, a work of literature resonates with a reader's experience in just such a way that the event of reading reaches us with the force of saturated phenomenality regardless of what we have or have not done to prepare ourselves. Other times, however, receiving the force of a work requires mental preparation. If the imagined student sitting in the back three seats to the right had made an effort to hope that a poem could rattle his preconceptions and awaken some awareness in him, then he would have heard Randall's poem differently. In cultivating a willingness to be

---

[20] Marion, *Erotic Phenomenon*, 89.

overwhelmed by the event of reading literature, we cultivate an ability to hope without condition in the overwhelming arrival of the beloved.

The repeated reading of the same book offers a special case of the event of reading. Even if we have read the book before, each experience of reading offers new pleasures, but sometimes the pleasure we seek in a favorite book is the not-newness. Even the experience of surprise or exaltation can unfold in a double-minded way where we look forward to the surprise or heightened effect. We expect it. We do not prepare a place for the reading event's appearance without condition, as true hope would, but we prepare a place open enough for the text to sweep us away just like it has before. Reciting *Childe Harold's Pilgrimage* ("There is a pleasure in the pathless woods") with students on top of Helm Crag in the Lakes District, I expected to be exalted. I expected us to all feel a little silly. I expected the lines to have greater resonance for the now-sweaty city kids than it had ever had before. All of these things happened as expected, but the event was nevertheless saturated well beyond the level of common law phenomenality.

A final point should be made about reading as event. Hopeful reading, like hopeful loving, can be painful. The reading event that brings with it the force of saturated phenomenality can overwhelm us with pain as well as pleasure. In his exploration of *The Witness of Poetry*, Czeslaw Milosz explains that "only an awareness of the dangers menacing what we love allows us to sense the dimension of time and to feel in everything we see and touch the presence of past generations."[21] Each reader brings to a reading a different awareness of what has menaced love as well as different loves. Consequently, a reader who has experienced the traumatic and sudden loss of a child, will experience "Ballad of Birmingham" with a more charged awareness of the fragility of life in the face of menacing violence. The poem may open a conduit to a remembered event that overwhelms the awareness of the poem entirely. Such an event, for all its saturation, may be neither pleasant nor beneficial. Although the ability to be overwhelmed by a work of literature generally supports readers' attempts to love other people unconditionally, reading associated with a traumatic event can re-enliven a remembered experience that gets in the way of love.

---

[21] Czeslaw Milosz, *The Witness of Poetry* (Cambridge: Harvard University Press, 1983), 4.

Conversely, poetry connected to overwhelming life events can benefit a reader by moving a memory whose recurrence is overwhelming closer to something like a common-law phenomenon. Sometimes a work of literature's benefit operates by offering categories through which one *can* contain and more carefully approach the memory of trauma. In such a case, the greatest benefit of a saturated event of reading is that it will reduce the level of saturation of future events of memory. The poetry circulated in newspapers for soldiers during the American Civil War provides an example of poetry that served the cause of love by making experience *more* containable.[22] This is a special case, however. Most of us have plenty of practice rendering events predictable through the mobilization of our expectations beforehand. What we need practice in, in order to grow as lovers, is the willingness to be overwhelmed.

Reading as idol

Although Marion treats all saturated phenomena as events, he has a more specific formulation of the event of viewing a painting. He discusses painting as idol, "the first visible that sight cannot pierce and abandon, because it … hoards up all admiration in it." As idol, the painting "returns to the look its proper measure, of which it was not aware, until then not having had enough of what is visible."[23] This is a curious figure in that Marion describes the look becoming aware of itself by realizing its boundaries. This must refer to the self-reflective process of the ego realizing the boundaries of the look, but separating the look from the ego is problematic within the erotic reduction since the ego is constituted through activity, including the activity of looking. Viewing the painting overwhelms us as other events do, but in hoarding our admiration, the painting as idol also centralizes the origin of the intuition that overwhelms us. It thus gives us something to contemplate as the source of our bedazzlement in a way that other events do not. Looking at paintings (or readings as I will

---

[22] See Elizabeth Lorang, "Not Feeling Very Well … We Turned our Attention to Poetry: Poetry, Hospital Newspapers, and the Civil War," *Literature and Journalism: Inspiration, Intersections, and Inventions from Ben Franklin to Stephen Colbert*, ed. Mark Canada (Basingstoke: Palgrave, 2013).

[23] Marion, *In Excess*, 61.

go on to argue) foregrounds the act of looking and increases our awareness of it as an element of phenomenality. The awareness of our power to look, which threatens to become mere self-contemplation, is rescued by the power of the painting itself, which draws the viewer back to it. The experience of being struck by a painting and not wanting to "abandon" looking resembles the experience of being struck by a book and not wanting to abandon it for the everyday rituals of eating and sleeping that try to call us away.

Looking at a painting differs from simply seeing it, in Marion's description, in that the look is active. It seeks what the painting presents in order to find what it excludes. It follows shapes that interact and balance each other or recognizes colors that seize light.[24] Looking actively in this way is both receptive and restrictive. The painting's ability to hoard admiration and increase our awareness of the act of looking depends on two factors related to the look's reception of a painting. First, the look's ability to receive the painting depends on the painting's stillness. In the still moment of looking, the event of viewing is drawn out in a way that saturated phenomena outside of art rarely allow. Mothers watch their children sleeping because they are rarely otherwise still enough to see. The bird that perches leaf-like in a bare tree flies away before its admirer can perceive the balance of the shape it might have created. Looking at art is a privileged example of saturated phenomenality because the viewer determines the temporality of the event of looking in a way that she cannot for other events.

Second, the painting makes all of itself visible to the viewer, something that objects in the world cannot do. The cube provides the standard example for this problem in phenomenology, but the lions in Trafalgar Square provide a less abstract instance. If I look at the sculptures of lions in Trafalgar Square, I cannot see them at one time. I have to walk all the way around the base in order to experience each side and then imagine them as a whole. Every side that the sculpture presents to me implies but fails to reveal an a-presentable side.[25] A painting, however, makes itself fully visible to the viewer. In describing the icon, Marion will differentiate the unseen backside of the lions (in my

---

[24] Marion, *In Excess*, 55–56.

[25] For Marion's version of this problem, see *In Excess*, 62–63. For Husserl's, see *Paris Lectures*, trans. Peter Koestenbaum (Dordrecht: Springer, 1964), 16–18.

example), an unseen that can be intended, from the unseen that definitively exceeds visibility and cannot be intended. The exemplary instance of this later is the icon, the face of the other. Marion defines the idolatrous look in contrast to the iconic look. The icon substitutes "its own aim—its aim toward us—in place of ours toward it".[26] Books possess both kinds of invisibility in that they unfold across time, each page becoming visible in its turn, and in that they imply an invisible world that we can participate in but never fully intend. As will be seen in considering the icon, however, books like paintings only achieve the rank of the icon in the unique circumstance of prayerful reading or viewing because otherwise they only appear to direct an intentionality toward us. That intentionality is the product of their actual visibility (words on pages) rather than a look originating elsewhere that could be revoked. Books cannot choose to not be read, but a human other can choose to turn away. In spite of books' temporal unfolding and the consequent impossibility of seeing them all at one time, they share with painting the ability to concentrate overwhelming givenness in one still source. A reader can look again and again at a beautiful page or even a beautiful temporal structure created by the text in the same way that she can return again and again to a juxtaposition of colors in a painting.

A painting may represent something realistically and a viewer imagine another side to it, but he knows that the other side is an illusion, and that the visible as presented is all there is to see. The painting's visibility thus differs from that of a cube not only in the paucity of what it offers—no unseen other side—but also in the fecundity of what it might imply constricted within a frame. Imagining the world of a painting involves far more that seeing the other side. This is most obvious in representational painting, but is true for all painting, as more abstract works refer to modes of seeing or not seeing that they do not include within their own frame. Heidegger illustrates this available excess of implication in his meditation on one of Van Gogh's paintings of peasant shoes:

> From the dark opening of the worn insides of the shoes, the toilsome tread of the worker stares forth. In the stiffly rugged heaviness of the shoes there is the accumulated tenacity of her slow trudge through the far-spreading and ever uniform furrows of the field swept by a raw wind.... This equipment is

---

[26] Marion, *Crossing*, 33.

pervaded by uncomplaining worry as to the certainty of bread, the wordless joy of having once more withstood want.[27]

Heidegger here allows Van Gogh's painting to summon the world of a peasant woman's daily life. The painting enables and shapes the contemplation of what it does not represent. What Heidegger is doing here, though, is contemplating more than looking. He is thematizing the imagined life of the woman who might have worn these shoes, rather than letting the painting itself hold his admiration. He announces that he is only examining a "sort of useful article"— shoes not paintings—so I am not accusing Heidegger of anything he does not acknowledge himself. Nevertheless, it is Van Gogh's specific painting of shoes that brings forth this contemplation.

The painting invites the sort of contemplation Heidegger performs, but of course his is not the only way of looking at the painting. Derrida regards the same painting and sees something quite different. For him, there is no relationship between the shoes a human being might wear and their painted image other than the relationship that the painting forces by stitching the two together metaphorically (the image stands for shoes but is not). He finds this passage in Heidegger "naïve." Derrida contends that the painting does not, even in a metonymic form, represent the life of the woman who might have worn these shoes. Rather, "the frame makes a work of supplementary *désœuvrement*. It cuts out but also sews back together" the world out of which these shoes might have come and the formal elements of the painting itself. He uses the figure of the lace to describe the relationship between the painting and its milieu. The painting, by "an invisible lace which pierces the canvas," sews itself "back onto its milieu, onto its internal and external worlds."[28] Within the painting itself, Derrida discovers a figure that describes the action of the painting as such. The figure of the lace also provides him with the shape of his own essay, which weaves together excerpts from Heidegger's meditation on Van Gogh's shoes and Meyer Schapiro's "The Still Life as a Personal Object—a Note on Heidegger and van Gogh."

---

[27] Heidegger, "The Origin of the Work of Art," 159.
[28] Jacques Derrida, "Restitutions of the Truth in Pointing," in *The Art of Art History: A Critical Anthology*, ed. Donald Preziosi (Oxford: Oxford University Press, 2009).

Different as these acts of looking are, they are both idolatrous in Marion's formulation. Describing what the painting reveals, Marion says, "Name your idol and you will know what you are"; in reflecting the shape of the viewer's capacity to look, the painting behaves like a mirror.[29] The viewer sees himself. Neither Heidegger nor Derrida "name their idol" in their descriptions of looking at Van Gogh's *A Pair of Shoes*. That is to say, neither of them writes that he is writing about his own way of viewing, but both philosophers make available (for their own viewing or their reader's) the shape of their desire as viewers. Heidegger, ultimately interested in shoes and not paintings, lets Van Gogh's painting speak to him of shoes and then follows what the painting has suggested into a contemplation of a peasant woman. Derrida, ultimately interested in discovering a figure within the painting that will overcome what he sees as the naiveté and logocentrism of Heidegger's reading, lets the painting give him the figure of laces and pointing or pricking and sewing. "The idol" thus "remains, in one way or another, proportionate to the expectations of the desire ... [I]t fulfills (sometimes to a degree more than expected) the anticipation."

The painting or work of literature as idol is always a mirror for the viewer or reader's desire, but since two forces are at play—what the work of art offers and what the viewer or reader receives—one can think distinctly about the effect of the work's invitation and the effect of the viewer's receptivity. In addition to being receptive, the look is also restrictive. It constrains the visibility of the painting: to look means "to manage the excess of the visible."[30] In managing the excess of the visible, the look can expand only to the limits of the viewer's capacity. Receptivity can be limited by aesthetic competence as well as incompetence or inattention. At times, the critic may look intently at the work, in just the way Marion describes—following the lines, sounding out the tonal resonances—and not reach the boundaries of her own looking. It may be the case that the most powerful lookers are in fact the most resistant to letting a work of art shape their act of looking. What they see without exceeding the bounds of their own aperture is already so vast that they are content. They have farther to go to see the boundaries of their own capacity to see.

---

[29] Marion, *In Excess*, 61.
[30] Marion, *In Excess*, 57.

When we are receptive, the idol "liberates our gaze from objectivity."[31] This is evident in Heidegger and Derrida's readings of Van Gogh's painting. The painting has set aside its shoes for the sake of visibility, not so that they can be seen in a way that joins intention and intuition seamlessly as happens with common-law phenomena, but so that their image can give something more. The painting confesses its inadequacy to the life that the shoes have borne, but the shoes themselves, the objects represented, have no claim to adequate presentation of life either. What we see when we see them in Van Gogh's painting is the gap between an implied experience of life (the life Heidegger imagines perhaps, but also many more) and that experience's material remains. The painting is itself the remains of such a process. As Wassily Kandinsky writes, "Each painting mysteriously contains an entire life, a life of many sufferings, hours of doubts, of enthusiasm and of delighted inspiration. Whither does this life go?"[32] It does not, it cannot go into the painting. But the painting points to this inadequacy as a property of visuality itself. It reminds viewers of all that exceeds and confounds visibility by expanding to the limits of visibility.

Literature does this as well. It functions idolatrously in that it brings the viewer's gaze to life, and not just her gaze, but her full sensual potential, through the taste of water in McCarthy's *The Crossing* or the smell of yams in Ellison's *Invisible Man*. As with paintings, however, a work of literature points to everything it is not, everything imagined but not present and everything that exceeds our capacity to imagine. The scene of the *Invisible Man* smelling yams is a case in point. The text is sensually replete. As the narrator walks the winter streets of Harlem he sees through one window "plaster images of Mary and Jesus surrounded by dream books" and through another "switches of wiry false hair, ointments guaranteed to produce the miracle of whitening black skin. 'You too can be truly beautiful,' a sign proclaimed,'" but juxtaposed against these proclaiming images is the vacuousness of the street itself where he hears only "the fall of snow upon snow."[33] He is looking for a place to sleep

---

[31] Marion, *Crossing*, 33 and 41.
[32] Wassily Kandinsky, *On the Spiritual in Art*, ed. and trans. Hilla Rebay (New York: Guggenheim Foundation, 1946), 12.
[33] Ralph Ellison, *Invisible Man* (New York: Vintage, 1995), 262.

when he is awakened from both the loud alienation of the images and the silent loneliness of the street. Farther along on a corner

> a stove pipe reeled off a thin spiral of smoke that drifted the odor of baking yams slowly to me bringing a stab of swift nostalgia. I stopped as though struck by a shot, deeply inhaling, remembering, my mind surging back, back. At home we'd bake them in the hot coals of the fireplace, had carried them cold to school for lunch; munched them secretly, squeezing the sweet pulp from the soft peel as we hid from the teacher, behind the largest book, the *World's Geography*.[34]

The narrator recalls that "time seemed endlessly expanded, stretched thin as the spiraling smoke, beyond all recall." Time has extended beyond its representation in years. Geography has become a relationship of place to a person and a culture, something that no book, however big, could document. As he bites into his yam, the narrator turns away from the old man who has sold it to him to hide his emotion, and as he walks, he becomes exhilarated "by an intense feeling of freedom." He remembers a time when he would have been ashamed to eat food associated with the South in Harlem, "trying to do only what was expected" of him instead of what he "had wished to do."

Then the novel takes a sudden turn. What seems to have been a progression from the empty promise of appearances (images in the windows) to the substance of physical reality and grounded identity (yams) moves to a third stage where image and the grounding of identity in physical and memorial selfhood come together in an eviction. The narrator almost trips over the evicted "junk." He cannot bear to look at the evicted couple themselves, but their dispossessed possessions compel him to look: a portrait, a Bible, shabby chairs, the husband's note freeing him from slavery. The evicted woman says repeatedly, "Just look, just look." What the narrator sees, finally, is "no longer what was before my eyes, but inwardly-outwardly, around a corner into the dark far-away-and-long-ago, not so much of my own memory, as of remembered worlds, linked verbal echoes, images heard even when not listening at home."[35] He sees his mother's hands hanging laundry "white and

---

[34] Ellison, *Invisible Man*, 262.
[35] Ellison, *Invisible Man*, 273. Sara Blair reads this scene in relation to visuality as well, but she focuses on the role of textual and pictorial documentation of a shared black history. See her "Ellison,

raw in the skirt-swirling wind." When he begins to speak to the now gathered crowd a few pages later, what he looks for and cannot see is the labor of the eighty-seven-year-old evicted man. The whole passage, right at the center of the novel, moves between what the book can represent and all the things that it can only gesture toward. It calls on all the senses—the cold of his mother's hands, the smell of the yams, the sound of the snow, the images trapped behind their window—to try and conjure something that sense cannot deliver. And it foregrounds the narrator's movement between the sensual promptings of a Harlem street and the evocations given through those promptings. The novel sets off a subsequent series of seeking the invisible in the reader whose own "remembered worlds" give these flimsy pages their power. In charting the contours of these remembered worlds and the contours of the world that *Invisible Man* opens up, the reader approaches the text as idol. There is no counter-intentional gaze that opposes the reader, but the reader discovers a power of looking that our lives outside of books do not often call attention to.

Marion's use of the term "idol" suggests the power that he grants painting, but also alludes to the circularity of self-congratulatory encounters with art where a viewer admires her ability to flex her aesthetic muscles for her own pleasure more than engaging the work itself. That is not to say that Marion condemns viewing painting as idol. The process of being revealed to ourselves through art has a great deal of latent power. In ushering the painting into visibility, the painter performs an ethical act. "Art bears the responsibility of what it gives to see and, even further, the responsibility of its power to make us look.[36] Since the viewer's capacity to look shapes the phenomenon of the painting's appearance, the act of looking shares this ethical responsibility. For the critic, whose look will guide the looking of others, this responsibility is multiplied. As an idol, the painting's power arises from the challenge that it issues: can the viewer prove herself adequate to the painting's visibility? Can her desire sustain itself long enough to take in all the painting has to offer? The answer is always no. But, the effort changes our ability to look and desire in a way that no other singular instance of visibility could have. A critic who allows her look to be expanded

---

Photography and the Origins of Invisibility" in *The Cambridge Companion to Ralph Ellison* (Cambridge: Cambridge University Press, 2005).

[36] Marion, *In Excess*, 61.

in an encounter with a text and who recognizes the new limits of her look exposed through the encounter with a work of art models a willingness to be overwhelmed. That willingness to be overwhelmed is a crucial element in one's ability to love and be loved, so even if another intentionality is not evoked through an idolatrous reading or looking, the evolving self becomes aware of its own porousness in a way that strengthens her capacity to love.

Reading as icon

Idolatrous reading cannot move beyond the space between a reader and a text. That space is already humming with possibilities, but it is not everything, particularly not for Marion, who is a Catholic. To exceed the bounds of the space between painting and viewer or reader and text, Marion turns to the concept of the icon. An iconic look is prayerfully addressed to Christ, and it proceeds in the faith that Christ will look back, countering the intentionality of the seeker with his own intentionality. This pattern of crossed intentionalities and its associated image of the crossed gaze become for Marion the basis of his articulation of the saturated phenomenon of the icon.

The icon, the third mode of saturated phenomenality discussed here, is saturated according to modality. Not only do individual instances of the icon overflow our intentionality; the icon can never even be intended and our experience of it is always characterized by that fact. Marion discusses two forms of invisibility—that which our intention can aim at but that we never can receive adequately through intuition (such as the Trafalgar Square lions that one cannot see all sides of), and that which defies intention from the start. His paradigmatic example of this second category is the face. When I turn to regard my little boy, what meets my gaze is his gaze, a counter-intentionality that could not even be imagined as expressible. In the act of looking at each other, we experience being seen as well as seeing.

Literature behaves as both event and idol when conceived as an act of reading or a stable artistic object, respectively. It can also be approached as icon. The concept of iconicity has changed in Marion's work over the past twenty-five years. *The Crossing of the Visible* (1991, trans. 2004) includes Marion's early theorization of the concepts of idol and icon. In *Crossing*, both idol and icon remain more connected to their theological moorings. They also are more aligned with the perspective of the viewer than with specific categories of phenomenality. Later, in *In Excess: Studies of Saturated Phenomena* (2001, trans. 2002), Marion articulates a more strictly phenomenological version of the idol and the icon.[37] While *In Excess* primarily expounds on the face of the human or divine other as icon, *The Crossing of the Visible* draws on a patristic tradition to make clear that painting, too, can be approached as icon. An iconic view of painting looks through the painting itself toward the invisible face of Christ. The painting effaces itself in this process, transferring the viewer's adoration to Christ without needing to transverse an imagined distance between visible and invisible. The viewer of a painted icon finds herself attended to by Christ. That Christic look breaks through the visible/invisible divide and pronounces the divide itself a metaphysical illusion. The viewer thereby experiences an exalted version of the reversal of intentionality experienced while gazing at another person.

Since the terms idol and icon describe ways of perceiving rather than objects perceived, both art and the face of the other can be regarded as idol or icon. We can look at the face of the other, which is properly speaking an iconic site of counter-intentionality, and idolize that other, seeing only ourselves. We can look at a work of art, regardless of what it presents, as idol or icon. The difference between the idol and the icon in art in its early formulation, then, is a matter of approach, but this approach should not be conceived as operating entirely under the control of a reader's will. It is invited by the work of art, and the same work will issue its invitation to viewers and readers in differing ways.

The apparently panoptic idea of being looked at through a piece of art will likely alienate some readers, but Marion argues that the experience of God should not be set outside of the phenomena examined as part of human experience because to shut it out would be to foreclose phenomenological

---

[37] Significantly, Dominique Janicaud published *Le Tournant théologique de la phénoménologie française* in 1991, charging Marion with smuggling theology into phenomenological work. Michael Henry, Emmanual Lévinas, and Jean-Louis Chrétien were similarly accused. For the translation of Janicaud's accusation and responses to it, see Dominique Janicaud, Jean-Francois Courtine, Jean-Louis Chrétien, Michel Henry, Jean-Luc Marion, and Paul Ricoeur, *Phenomenology and the Theological Turn: The French Debate.* (New York: Fordham, 2001).

possibility on a non-phenomenological basis (usually an empirical basis). This leads to the question of what other possibilities are unceremoniously shut out of most critical practice. Eve Kosofsky-Sedgwick pointed out in *Touching Feeling* that sometime between Paul Ricoeur's coining of the phrase in 1970 and the turn of the twenty-first century, the "hermeneutics of suspicion" went from being one possibility among others in a taxonomy of critical practices to "a mandatory injunction."[38] Suspicion, a rarely named affective stance that masquerades as a critical imperative, simply forbids reference to a beyond (beyond empiricism, beyond the text itself, beyond the tissue of carefully rewoven historical ideologies). Rita Felski puts the problem succinctly in her recent reflections on "Critique and the Hermeneutics of Suspicion."

> [C]ritique often chafes at the presence of other forms of thought. Ruling out the possibility of peaceful co-existence or even mutual indifference, it insists that those who do not embrace its tenets must be denying or disavowing them. In this manner, whatever is different from critique is turned into the photographic negative of critique—evidence of an irrefutable lack or culpable absence. To refuse to be critical is to be uncritical.[39]

Felski points out that critique reproduces itself so effectively that discourses that claim to challenge its suspicious affective tonality end up being co-opted. It is just too ideologically dominant to contest head on. One ends up arguing for a critique of critique, reinforcing its norms of practice rather than opening another way.

Even if critical practice could be opened to less suspicious ways of reading based, perhaps, on the increasing attention to embodied experience within literary and cultural studies, or based on the renewed attention to affect, could it open its practices broadly enough to include the possibility of iconic reading, reading that proceeds confidently in the possibility of revelation? Marion's definition of the icon, at least in its earliest formulations, signals such a possibility.[40] The clear theological underpinnings of *The Crossing of the Visible*

---

[38] Eve Kosofsky-Sedgwick, *Touching Feeling: Affect, Pedagogy, Performativity* (Durham: Duke University Press, 2003), 125.

[39] Rita Felski, "Critique and the Hermeneutic of Suspicion," *M/C Journal: A Journal of Media and Culture* 15, no. 1 (2012).

[40] Marion himself performs a reading of St. Augustine's *Confessions* as icon in Jean-Luc Marion, *In the Self's Place: The Approach of St. Augustine*, trans. Jeffrey L. Kosky (Stanford: Stanford University Press, 2012).

may trouble some critics since Christianity refers to a discourse viewed, on the one hand, as historically dominant and complicit with the violence of the West and on the other, to a range of practices aligned with peace-making and a receptive regard for human others and the divine.

Marion's later identification of the icon with the face of the other offers another alternative to the hermeneutics of suspicion, one that requires a less radical departure from widespread critical practices. Using the face as the figure of counter-intentionality, Marion works out an idea that will become essential for his later articulation of the erotic reduction—the importance of counter-intentionality in the formation of the never-really-independent self. We depend on that which is definitively outside ourselves for assurance that we can be loved, and we require that assurance to go on living. Without the possibility of revelation through art (a possibility in traditional practices of iconic prayer), the relationship between the engagement with art as icon and the engagement with the face as icon takes on a metaphorical rather that a metonymic relationship because art no longer offers a means through which to be assured that we are loved. Outside of a view that accepts iconicity, however, a work of art may still be approached as something sharing with other people an ability to change the viewer and an endless hermeneutical potential. Engaging a painting, poem, or novel then becomes *like* engaging another person except for two important differences. First, a work of art may resist a viewer's intentionality, but it does not issue a counter-intentionality. Second, paintings and books do not have flesh. Art's lack of intentionality and flesh throws us back into the arms of human others. The experience of an endless hermeneutic as art can offer it, which is to say without the accompanying experience of being assured that we can be loved, highlights the need for that assurance all the more.

Reading and the flesh

The final saturated phenomena discussed here is the flesh, which is saturated according to relation. There is no escaping the experience of the flesh, imaginatively or literally. The flesh gives us to ourselves by facilitating our interaction with the rest of the world and other people. Books have a body—they have a physical presence we can touch—but they lack flesh. In this distinction, "flesh" refers to the sensing body, through which we find the shape of who we are and experience life, and "body" refers to the thing-ness that we corporeally share with non-sensing things like trees and pencils.[41] The flesh is also that through which we love, and in order to claim that love through books affects love with other people, we have to recognize, paradoxically, that it is the exclusion of the flesh from books that makes an understanding of the flesh essential for understanding the relationship of love and reading. Because love requires flesh, and we require love, books can never provide the assurance necessary for the ego's continuance. It is our reliance on the flesh of others that propels a reader-in-love into the world of embodied others where love can be enacted in the flesh. Reading, as this book argues overall, can help strengthen us as lovers by enhancing our ability to attend to and empathize with the other and by enhancing our willingness to be overwhelmed. But reading can never give us love's assurance.

As a lot of recent writing about the body in literary criticism has shown, that does not mean that the consideration of the body is irrelevant for thinking about the phenomenon of reading a work of literature. The thingness of the body and its susceptibility to coding though performance and the observation of others have received particular attention lately. This is a different view of the body than what phenomenology proposes. The body as a site of cultural inscription collapses the distinction between body and flesh and focuses instead on the distinction between the body as the site of subjective experience and the body as the object of sociocultural construction. This subject/object distinction does not hold within a phenomenological view, particularly within a phenomenology of love that sees love between en-fleshed people as prior to any form of self-conception that would produce the illusion of independent subjectivity. During the height of critical-theoretical writing about the body, Terry Eagleton wryly caricatured the difference between the flesh conceived phenomenologically and new theoretical reflection, saying: "For Merleau-Ponty, the body is 'where there is something to be done'; for the new somatics,

---

[41] Marion, *In Excess*, 84.

the body is where something—gazing, imprinting, regimenting—is being done to you."[42]

Conceived phenomenologically, flesh translates "the given into a phenomenon. Outside my flesh, there is no phenomenon for me ... I cannot separate myself from my flesh."[43] The flesh saturates our intentionality in a different way than the event, the idol, and the icon, since it shapes intentionality in such a non-negotiable way. One can imagine trying (if not succeeding) to block out an event that one is witness to. We constantly negotiate the otherwise bewildering flow of events by receiving different simultaneously occurring events with differing levels of intentionality. One can imagine walking by a painting in a museum and not engaging it as idol or walking by one in a church and not engaging it as icon. The flesh gives rise to our intentionality, however. It shapes our imagination (one cannot imagine the Northern Lights, for example, without either having seen them or having heard them described). There is no imagining without the flesh and no escape from the flesh that does not take the form of an en-fleshed imagination. I could imagine being taller or warmer or imagine being someone who liked vodka drinking vodka, but at every turn, I find myself imagining an altered flesh and the experiences such a flesh could provide in terms of the flesh I already live through.

The flesh itself is absolutely given. One cannot decide not to have cancer or decide not to age. It is also the means through which we interact with all the rest of what is given in the world, including things that physically resist us, like the chair a reader sits on, those things that have only an imagined physical presence to attend to like the Invisible Man's yam, and those things which defy formal intentionality altogether such as the intention of another person. This phenomenological flesh has not received much literary critical attention,[44] but it deserves to because of its bedrock importance to reader's imaginative and aesthetic experiences and because of literature's paradoxical relationship to the flesh. Literature not only operates without flesh. It gains its freedom to

---

[42] Terry Eagleton, "It Is Not Quite True That I Have a Body, and Not Quite True That I Am One Either," review of Peter Brooks's *Body Work*, *London Review of Books* 15, no. 10 (1993).

[43] Marion, *In Excess*, 89.

[44] Jessica Wiskus's *The River of Thought: Literature and Music after Merleau-Ponty* offers an interesting trans-disciplinary exception (Chicago: University of Chicago Press, 2015).

operate by means of its fleshlessness. It lives "only by evading the incarnation it puts into play."[45] Literature must exceed the confines that flesh would impose on it for a reader to imagine that the voice of a first-person narrator refers to a potential experience of the reader's flesh when referring to events that occurred to the flesh that the text projects him as having. It is literature's ability to exceed the flesh that allows a reader to imagine experiencing another flesh. The identification of a reader with a character or narrator is never complete and never free from questions about the confines that our own en-fleshed experiences impose on an act of reading, but the fact that such identification happens at all recalls literature's ability to put incarnation "into play."

Literature fuels a utopian political and personal imagination through its ability to evoke an incarnation it does not possess. The most extreme physical descriptions illustrate this most clearly. Descriptions of cold, hunger, or violence awaken a reader (who is not desensitized) to the physical capacity for suffering he shares with someone of another time or place. Ethical claims about the potential of such imaginative sharing of suffering could easily be exaggerated, but the shared contingency of human flesh offers a powerful reminder of the human commonalities that compete with cultural differences. This is not to say that the body exists prior to its cultural construction. A hermeneutics of the body has begun by the time we realize we have bodies, but part of that hermeneutic is the realization that others resemble us in their corporeality and fragility. The self-contained-ness of my body creates the illusion that I am independent, but its fragility reminds me that I am not. Literature can therefore shore up the boundaries of an illusory self, conceived as independent, by conveying to the reader the sense of having the sole privilege of viewing a world or mind that does not view him back. But, one book or poem can create this illusion thousands of times through the enfleshed act of seeing (or hearing) words and letting them transform themselves into imagined kitchens or precipices or snowstorms. That shared miracle of imagining with a text depends on, not just a body, but a flesh, and the sharedness of a text reminds a reader that the boundaries of the self the body seems to suggest are an illusion.

---

[45] Jacques Rancière, *The Flesh of Words: The Politics of Writing*, trans Charlotte Mandell (Stanford: Stanford University Press, 2004), 5.

The power of literature (and written communication more broadly) to evoke the experience of the flesh invites the question of whether the flesh is after all necessary for love. At times, Marion assumes that we can love someone who is not physically present. Does this imply that we can fully accomplish the erotic phenomenon with a book, which in many ways resembles the subjectivity of another person? Up to this point, I have assumed that the flesh is necessary for love, but this assumption should be investigated more closely. Scholars have accused Marion of positing a love that does not tend to our embodied existence enough,[46] implying that, in his definition, love does not require enfleshed activity at all. Such an accusation must be cleared up if I am to argue that books propel the lover back toward embodied people. The accusation that Marion proposes a fleshless love arises from his description of a non-signifying erotic speech, which gives the other flesh through speech alone (*EP* 148). Before concluding this chapter, I consider whether the instances Marion mentions of love without the presence of two bodies and two fleshes indicate a more general possibility that love can be fully accomplished without the encounter of the conjoined flesh.

Discussing how we love when our beloved is away, Marion argues against the possibility of auto-eroticization, saying, "I affect myself without exception, in my own flesh, through the other" even if "I imagine her.... [T]he absent one remains ever present, with an irreducible and indispensable alterity, even when the alterity remains simply fantasized" (*EP* 123). This sounds at first like an instance of love through the imagination alone. We can think here of Abelard and Heloise, loving each other through letters and through imagination. We could even think of the daily separation of running off to work or school or play. We love through those daily absences. In a particularly beautiful passage in *The Erotic Phenomenon*, Marion writes, "The lover never finishes telling himself of the beloved, telling himself to the beloved, and telling the beloved to herself" (210). The first of these actions—telling oneself of the beloved—carries on when we are alone. But these times of loving the other by oneself follow and precede moments of embodied love. Never reaching completion because they are created as they create us, our loving relationships are forever

---

[46] See John Milbank, "The Gift and the Mirror," *Counter-Experiences: Reading Jean-Luc Marion*, ed. Kevin Hart (Notre Dame, IN: University of Notre Dame Press, 2007); and Tóth, "Love Between Embodiment and Spirituality."

renewing themselves in the face of absence as long as we both love. If the beloved-in-person is temporarily absent, the lover can, in a way, make love through narrative. He can tell himself of the beloved. But narrative alone is not enough. The beloved-in-the-flesh returns and overflows the lover's story.

The death of the beloved provides another, more radical, example of love that continues in spite of bodily absence. Marion states quite clearly that "if the other is dead, I can, as lover, still love her, since I can love without reciprocity" (*EP* 193). Indeed, to love at all, we must love without hope of reciprocity. And although through the death of the beloved we lose the possibility of renewing the erotic reduction in the flesh, we remain, by having loved, secure within it. We are always still the self that the other gave us through his or her flesh. Marion writes, lovers "do not promise one another eternity, they provoke it and give it to one another starting now" (*EP* 209). All acts of love are already eternal. This is possible because, unlike the ontological reduction, the erotic reduction does not "belong to the horizon of being" (*EP* 193). So even when the beloved has passed beyond the edge of being, he or she remains secure within the boundary of love. Marion even privileges love beyond death as the most forceful realization of "the other as the saturated phenomenon *par excellance*," because "only the one who has lived with the life and the death of another person knows to what extent he or she does not know the other."[47]

In the final, most radical example, love through bodily absence, Marion discusses the love of God. God reveals himself in his very self as "the one and only love, that which we also practice" (*EP* 221). And crucially, Marion follows God's love through the same steps in the erotic reduction that we follow with our neighbors and beloveds, including a kind of crossing of the flesh. At the end of *The Erotic Phenomenon*, he writes that God "plays the lover, like us— passing through vanity (idols), the request that one love him and the advance to love first, the oath and the face (the icon), the flesh and the enjoyment of communion, the pain of our suspension and the jealous demand, the birth of the third party in transit and the announcement of the eschatological third party, who ends up by identifying himself in the incarnated Son" (221–222). The Eucharist is here represented as the mutual moment of embodied commitment

---

[47] Marion, *In Excess*, 126.

to the other, wherein the recipient recognizes that she receives herself through the body of Christ. One wonders if the bread and wine here stand in the same relation to the crucifixion and resurrection as speech does to the crossing of the flesh, if that which we take as the body and the blood gains importance by losing signification, adequate signification of love and God both being impossible. Regarding the relationship between speech and the flesh, Marion writes that "every great suffering, and thus every true climax remain mute" because there are not words to signify the erased phenomenon of what has just passed (*EP* 144). However, following the crossing of the flesh, my lover and I have become "partners of a privilege of worldly inexistence," and we speak to affirm this partnership "even though we speak of nothing" (*EP* 145). Similarly, in the Eucharistic crossing of the flesh, the content of what is said is empty, is even emptiness. It says jointly, "I give to you the body and blood that took flesh only to be given," and it refers back to Christ's most complete embodied self-giving.

In each of these three instances—the temporary absence or death of a beloved and the love of God—the crossing of the flesh marks the completion of the erotic phenomenon. Even if the beloved knows that such a crossing can never occur again, he or she remains permanently changed by the crossing that has happened. "I will never lose what I had to become" to love another (*EP* 188), whether we confirmed our love through an open conversation and handshake or through years of shared marital life. When Marion discusses making love through language, it is the language of lovers who have (just) completed the erotic reduction through the flesh (*EP* 135–150). That flesh may be distinguished from the body that gives rise to it, but cannot somehow break free of the body and inhabit ink and paper. If love depends on the flesh, as it does in every case, then it depends on our dear and fading bodies as well. Reading can be approached through three of the four categories of saturated phenomena, but the flesh remains separate, a privilege of embodied beloveds.

Love and the endless hermeneutic

Every book gives itself to us as a saturated phenomenon every time we read it—as an event that we cannot anticipate, fully embrace or remember, as an idol that we cannot command but that reveals our capacity to look, and possibly as an icon. Because books, through their use of language, approximate the way we think ourselves to ourselves, they also mimic the kind of interaction we have with other people. They come to us from elsewhere, inviting us to let our intention be overwhelmed by their intuition, which arises not as a simple object-given but as an occurrence shaped between the forces of our looking and their directing of that look. That is almost like a conversation, almost like encountering another person, except for two important differences. Books lack flesh, and they lack intentionality. Therefore, the responsibility that rises up between enfleshed people because of their shared fragility does not rise up between a reader and a book. Also, books may be shaped in the process of giving themselves by readers, but their embodied ink and paper form does not change in relation to readers because, unlike other people, they have no regard for us. They do not intend us.

Reading a book is an experience that unfolds through time, and is not capturable, or even recallable in one instant. A work of art, painting, or poem, "will never be a closed object, exhaustively seen," and in this it resembles another person.[48] The unpredictable encounters that works of literature offer us can prepare us for unpredictable encounters with other people. In part, this happens through their ability to expose us to other kinds of human experiences. This is an old, humanist argument for reading, but humanism is not a progressive science. This old argument still holds merit within the erotic reduction. Our ability to look expands through repeated encounters with different forms of art and through repeated encounters with the same work of art. The intentionality we turn toward a painting or a poem expands so that we can see more. Similarly, our ability to intend a beloved human other expands through encounters with different others and through repeated encounters with each beloved. This is not a matter of knowing more. It is a matter of the intentionality turned toward a work of art or a person. That intentionality will have been formed through the loves and hates it has encountered as well as through the other saturated phenomena it has helped to bring forth. Having read the narrator's experience of homesickness in *Invisible Man* will expand

---

[48] Marion, *In Excess*, 71.

my capacity to perceive homesickness in a beloved in person. This will happen all the more readily if I call the novel to mind, but even if I do not, if I let it saturate my intentionality when I read it, then it will have helped shape the intentionality that I now can turn to my homesick beloved in person.

Another way that encounters with art as saturated phenomena can prepare us for the saturated phenomenality of another person has to do not with the specific intuition that books or poems give to us, but with the simple fact that they give us more than we can take in. They habituate us to having our expectations blown apart. Regular open communications with others whom we love or hate does this as well, but because we do not have the flesh-born common responsibility with books that we do with other people, we are freer in reading to recognize the manner in which our horizons have been changed. No physical danger threatens us or our beloveds no matter how threatening the ideas in a book are. No need, no forward-driving conversation imposes a temporality counter to the one that will allow intuition through a book to come to us most fully. We can stop on page 262 of *Invisible Man* and contemplate the pseudo-Hegelaian movement between visual sensory overload, vacuous interiority, and memory-beclouded yam. In real life, had we somehow been privileged to the narrating character's experience, we would either have had to keep walking with him away from the yam seller, or would have had to watch him walk away. Reading, we can explore the event we have just read about and the event of reading itself and spend time being overwhelmed by it.

Marion, following Paul Ricoeur, characterizes the interpretive possibilities that saturated phenomena give rise to as "endless." He points out that "It is precisely be-cause of this surplus of intuition" uniquely present in saturated phenomena, "that we need hermeneutics.

> Why? Because hermeneutics is always an inquiry for further concepts: hermeneutics is generated when we witness an excess rather than a lack of information rather than its lack.... There, where the need of hermeneutics arises, it is completely impossible to imagine that we may get at any moment an adequate, final concept.[49]

---

[49] Jean-Luc Marion and Richard Kearney, "A Dialogue with Jean-Luc Marion," *Philosophy Today* 48, no. 1 (Spring 2004): 13.

A work of literature, therefore, offers endless interpretive possibilities, or more importantly, offers endless potential future engagements as readers themselves change. In the inquiry into love and reading, we are not concerned primarily with the possibility of producing endless interpretations from a limited text, the production of new truths, but rather with the possibility of reading changing people. Within the erotic reduction, the truths that might result from textual interpretation derive their significance from the role that they play in the re-creation of individuals through love.

The potential for re-creation through texts is as endless as their hermeneutical possibilities since most of us are changing all the time, not always beneficially through love, but somehow. "To be alive," as Marion says, "does not always means to live in a better way, or in a more exciting way, and so on; what to be means is rather the process of becoming not what you are but what you are not .... [O]ur being is first of all in its deepest root possibility rather than actuality."[50] Significantly, however, not everyone is alive in the way that Marion describes. One may exist in a kind of death-in-life wherein there is "no change, no improvement, not even decay for years" (18). Since it is not possible to be alive at all without learning new information, the actualization of the possibility latent within us must rely on something more than encountering new truths. There must also be a willingness for new truths to change us. A reader could potentially read a literary text and produce a lucid interpretation, but remain unchanged him or herself and therefore continue on within this death-in-life. In order to be changed by a text, a reader must be previously committed to more than just the possibility of endless interpretation. He must be committed to the life of endlessly changing being.

[50] Marion and Kearney, "A Dialogue," 18.

Conclusion

Books after Midnight

Of all things
Breaking the heart
At this hour—
The spine that bends
A little too far back.

Damon Falke

Most literary theory that argues that one person's reading can benefit another person has operated within either the epistemic or ontological reductions. This has limited what could be said on reading's behalf because these reductions imply a primarily cognitivist or autonomous self, a self that has been shown to be a product of specific forms of cultural imagining. Forms of selfhood built around cognitive accumulation or resolute commitment to being fit very nicely with the present culture of storing up resources and exerting will. An ethical criticism based on the epistemic reduction implies that if we can accumulate more knowledge about how we should behave, then we will behave that way. An ethical criticism based on the ontological reduction assumes that if we can make ourselves resemble more closely an ideal form of being, then we will benefit our neighbors through the process of our own moral perfection. But in both of these cases, the force that moves ethical change, is the unrecognized force of love. It is the relationship between the force of love and reading that I have tried to clarify. There are strong hermeneutical traditions based on epistemic and ontological foundations, but these traditions have sustained debilitating critiques. Marion's erotic reduction offers the potential for a new kind of hermeneutics that resists the implied acquisitiveness of cognitivism and the implied domination of ontology. It is an unreasonable kind of reading, that commits first to the prioritization of love in person and receptivity of text before it quite knows what it has gotten itself into.

Charitable reading, as I have called it, is not anti-reason or post-reason. It merely asks that we acknowledge how unreasonable we are, particularly in love. Many of the "little, nameless, unremembered acts of kindness and love" lyricized in Wordsworth's "Tintern Abbey" cannot be reasonably accounted for. Athos's rescues of Jakob Beer in *Fugitive Pieces* is not reasonable, nor is the torment Elie Wiesel finds in Auschwitz. Turning the focus from acts portrayed in books to the act of reading itself, who can say why one book becomes a favorite at a certain season of life or why the words that inspire us ring more loudly than the words in the line that follows? It is not quite the case, to quote Wordsworth again, that we murder to dissect the books we hold closest to us, but it is the case that something beyond the well-turned phrase or looming image fixes our attention. Passing the love of one work of literature on to other readers—via casual conversation, teaching, or writing—requires reason because these acts transpire in a public sphere where reason and understanding facilitate the sharing of ideas, but in the more private realms of late-at-night reading, waiting-room reading, book inscription, in the before-the-house-wakes-up reading we do, or the jotting of quotes into journals, more than reason moves us. Pretending that these kinds of reading can be tidily distinguished does not serve the reader inside or outside the academy very well. I conclude this book by discussing the ways that reading in love moves beyond reason and by suggesting that charitable reading, which seems a very private personal act, can effect public good and engage historicized quandaries because these goods and quandaries arise from a tangle of lives in love that precede them and precede us.

Unreasonable reading

Reading, particularly reading to teach or reading to write literary analysis, requires rigorous intellectual analysis and clarity about one's own judgment. It also requires a kind of organizational logic that can convert an event of reading into a ninety-minute lecture or six-thousand-word argument. Public acts of literary criticism communicate via reason in order to be understood. Yet, as Marion points out, we often love unreasonably. If we expect love in return, according to the logic of exchange, then we do not love at all. Rather, we must unreasonably commit to loving first "without any guarantee of assurance." And "in loving without reciprocity, the lover loves without reason.... He renounces reason and sufficiency" (*EP* 78, 79). How then can the unreasonableness of love be reconciled to the reason-demanding practices of reading? Reason is a primary source of the categories that would limit our experience of the event of reading. Therefore, it is reason more than anything that the saturated phenomenon of reading literature overwhelms. And yet, it would be absurd to propose that we could process language, image, argument, etcetera, without reason.

Marion clarifies the relationship of reason to love in person, and his clarification illuminates the role of reason in reading also. He says that "the issue is not ... a lack of reasoning or of good sense" on the part of the lover, "but rather a failure of reason itself to give reasons for the initiative to love." In other words, I may reason about my love, but I cannot reason my way into love. This is because love is a primary and not a secondary epistemology. "I do not love because I know what I see, but inversely I see and I know in the measure that I, the first to love, love" (*EP* 79–80). Charitable reading, according to Marion's characterization of love's own logic, begins with love and finds reasons afterward. Just as the person I love reveals himself to me in the light of that love and not prior to it, the book that I charitably read reveals itself to me more fully than one that I approach with reason alone. Marion uses the image of Orpheus trying to rescue Eurydice from the underworld to explain: "The other is phenomenalized in the exact measure according to which the lover loves him or her and, as an Orpheus of phenomenality, tears him or her from indistinction and makes him or her emerge from the depths of the unseen"

(*EP* 80). The text I read gains distinctiveness and visibility when I read in love. If I, like Orpheus, feel insecure without the confirmation of my reason and try to set my love of a work aside and see it objectively, then it flees back into its own object-ness and loses its saturated phenomenality.

An example of a poem that responds readily to charitable reading is e. e. cummings' own poetic illustration of love's unreasonable reason, "somewhere i have never travelled, gladly beyond." The poem begins by making its own statement about the singularity of any love experience:

> somewhere i have never travelled, gladly beyond
> any experience, your eyes have their silence:
> in your most frail gesture are things which enclose me,
> or which i cannot touch because they are too near[1]

Cummings's sense of the phenomenality of love anticipates Marion's in its emphasis on this moment of a shared lover's gaze being "beyond/ any experience." There is also a sense of the beloved other shaping the speaker's self as unnamable things in her gestures "enclose" him. The speaker presents himself as the recipient of a gift of love that he cannot make reasonable sense of because his lover's eyes retain "their silence." His own action of traveling with love is left syntactically incomplete in contrast to the self-sufficient syntax used to describe the silence of the beloved's eyes.

The poem continually emphasizes the speaker's inability to rationally understand love's operation upon him, but uses the language of openness to describe his willingness to let love proceed without yielding to understanding. In the second stanza he writes,

> your slightest look easily will unclose me
> though i have closed myself as fingers,
> you open always petal by petal myself as Spring opens
> (touching skilfully, mysteriously) her first rose

The third and fourth stanzas deny the sufficiency of rational conceptualization to contain love with the lines: "nothing which we are to perceive in this world

---

[1] Edward Estlin Cummings, *E. E. Cummings Complete Poems: 1904–1962*, ed. George J. Firmage (New York: Liveright, 1994), 97–98.

equals/ the power of your intense fragility" and "(i do not know what it is about you that closes/ and opens; only something in me understands." In spite of cummings's assertion here that "nothing in the world" equals the beloved's power, his imagery always seeks recourse to the things of the world. I quote the last three of the poem's five stanzas to illustrate the trend:

> or if your wish be to close me, i and
> my life will shut very beautifully, suddenly,
> as when the heart of this flower imagines
> the snow carefully everywhere descending;
>
> nothing which we are to perceive in this world equals
> the power of your intense fragility: whose texture
> compels me with the colour of its countries,
> rendering death and forever with each breathing
>
> (i do not know what it is about you that closes
> and opens; only something in me understands
> the voice of your eyes is deeper than all roses)
> nobody, not even the rain, has such small hands

The speaker compares himself to a flower, implying that this thing of the world is sufficient for describing him, but the beloved always outshines the natural phenomena to which she is compared. The rain is not as small as she is; roses cannot match her depth. Moreover, he luxuriates in the separate experiences that the beloved offers. He acknowledges her wholeness and the independence of her "wish," but describes her being revealed to him in experiences of a look that can be contemplated separately as sound (silence), action (unclose), a call (voice), or a touch (small hands). This imaginative variation on the multiple ways of experiencing her look attests to that look's unrecordability. The pairing of experiences that negate each other indicates that the experience of her look defies a logic of dichotomies. She can open like spring or close like snow, speak through silence or a voice, and her fragility renders (which can mean clarify, or produce) both "death and forever with each breathing."

All of this suggests that cummings offered a poetic description of love similar to Marion's phenomenological one a century earlier, but what is distinctive about a reading that receives cummings's poem through love and explains it through reason? How does such a reading differ demonstrably from a reading that approaches the poem through reason first? I will try to answer this question without lapsing into a dichotomy of reason and emotion that both Marion and cummings would refute. In attempting to do so, I am already allowing the poem's (and the philosopher's, in this case) phenomenality to overwhelm a reasonable distinction that could have been brought to bear upon it. This is an essential element of a reading that puts love before reason (since the question of the relationship between the two is a question of anteriority, not exclusion) —to allow the text to dictate the terms of our encounter with it. This practice initially seems similar to a Derridian practice of freeing the text from a reference or "presence" in the extra-textual world.[2] However, the Derridian practice frees some single sign or concept within the work for play among or against the rest of the work as a whole and makes the reader the puppet-master of that play. The practice I am recommending frees the text from referentiality to the objective extratextual world without presuming its separation from what Marion calls "the invisible." Marion suggests that we need art because it *adds* to the world of existence, not because it represents objects or events already present in the world.[3] The painter, and I would argue the author, is "a diviner." He or she is uniquely able to grant "visibility to the unseen." The artist works "in the obscure chaos (Genesis 1:2) that precedes the separation of the waters below and the waters above." He or she "goes back to the creation of the world"[4] and brings forth something that itself desired to be seen but that could not be found without the artist's divination.

The saturated phenomenality of the previously unseen that works upon the artist is then echoed in the saturated phenomenality of the work of art. It is significant that in both of these cases the artist and viewer or reader are conceived as recipients rather than creators. Both artist and viewer/reader try to keep themselves from anticipating what the work of art will offer. Marion

[2] Jacques Derrida, "Différance," trans. Alan Bass, *Margins of Philosophy* (Chicago: University of Chicago Press, 1982), 3–27. Here, Derrida argues that, typically, "when we cannot grasp or show the thing, state the present, the being-present, when the present cannot be presented, we signify, we go through the detour of the sign." He proposes that we instead put "into question the authority of presence" and liberate the sign for the play of meaning-creation during the act of reading.

[3] Marion, *Crossing*, 25.

[4] Marion, *Crossing*, 27–28.

calls the trap of anticipation "academicism" in painters, but it is no less recognizable in authors, critics, readers, and viewers of art. "Academicism (in art) consists only in this: claiming to foresee a painting, the painter prohibits the sudden appearing of the unseen and instead fixes its shape at first sight."[5] The language with which we discuss a poem necessarily brings a particular relationality among concepts; this cannot be avoided. Nevertheless, it is worth trying to receive concepts from a poem rather than impose them upon it. In the introduction to his *Collected Poems*, cummings writes, "Miracles are to come. With you I leave a remembrance of miracles." cummings's language here captures the wonder and newness of both artist and reader/viewer's experiences. Both experiences exceed the bounds of common phenomena and common reason in being "miraculous."

In addition to being unreasonably receptive to a book's givenness, charitable reading also turns a certain kind of intentionality toward a book. This intentionality is characterized by empathy and self-forgetful attention during the reading process, but is complemented by the more self-aware acts of contemplation and imaginative variation. The goal of such contemplation is not to locate and defend a single interpretation, but to allow multiple possible interpretations to emerge. The knowledge that is gained through this process I have called "knowing." Knowing includes not so much facts about as an awareness of. I do not learn *about* the Glanton gang reading *Blood Meridian*. If I wanted to confirm the historical facticity of the violent actions described in the novel, I would need to consult another source. What I learn, instead, is an enhanced and nuanced awareness of the capacity for violence that I share with other human beings. This awareness can itself give rise to any number of insights when thematized in relation to other works by McCarthy, other American novels from the 1980s or other works portraying characters who, like the Judge, reject empathy. An imaginative variation that follows these different routes of thematization would locate some boundaries of the text's hermeneutic potential, some interpretations that just do not make sense, but would also discern an endless number of possible readings in the background to the few it pursues. Such variation will, latently or knowingly, include the

[5] Marion, *Crossing*, 28.

interpretive acts of other readers since the book and all of its readers share a world. Reading within the erotic reduction will not predictably elevate one form of these possible interpretive acts above another. Readers in love will not, for example, always privilege the contemplation of texts exemplifying empathy's failure. But, individual readers in love will value their own contemplative (and critical and educative) acts in relation to love's primacy.

The situatedness of charitable reading

At first glance the argument that love provides the basis for all the value of literature seems profoundly ahistorical. Fredric Jameson wrote (already) in 1988 that "our entire contemporary social system has little by little begun to lose its capacity to retain its own past, has begun to live in a perpetual present and in a perpetual change that obliterates traditions of the kind which all earlier social formations have had in one way or another to preserve."[6] This was before the internet explosion and increase of global migration that have unaccountably accelerated the dehistoricizing effect of modern living. Because Marion's conception of love emphasizes the present, even the microscopic moment of sensual or aesthetic overwhelming, it might be argued that a theory of reading based in the erotic reduction participates in the obliteration of tradition that Jameson worries about. Perhaps, alone with a book, a reader inhabits a time apart, a private time separable from the communal time of shared historical progression. This is, in fact, what Marion implies about love in person. He argues that lovers give eternity to each other by reorienting the phenomenon of time in love making.

Ultimately, however, this view of love's temporality limits the power of love too much. The lovers, who might forget the history they share with more than just each other, and the reader, who disappears from shared time into the temporality of fiction, bring with them as part of themselves all the prior moments of the lives they share with many other people. We always love as one who has been loved before. We always read with other reading experiences

---

[6] Frederic Jameson, *The Cultural Turn: Selected Writings on the Postmodern, 1983–1998* (London: Verso, 1998), 20.

in us, shaping our approach to the present page. Moreover, we always read as someone situated squarely within personal and historical horizons of meaning. As Gramsci writes, "The starting-point of critical elaboration is the consciousness of what one really is, and is 'knowing thyself' as a product of the historical process to date which has deposited in you an infinity of traces, without leaving an inventory."[7] Within the erotic reduction, the crucial powers in history are love and hate, but history is still what we find ourselves in and what we contribute to making. One source of the variety of charitable readings is this historical situatedness. The love we make, being made uniquely possible by the people we encounter, is not possible for any other person. The responsibilities that love places on me as a lover in the flesh and a reader depend on the eccentric course of my own time-bound life. And so it is for every reader.

Reading literature carries us far enough to love first. In reading we yield our intentionality to a voice from outside our "egological sphere" (*EP* 102). The book we read provides second way of seeing that imitates the counter-intentionality of another person just enough to help us practice the initial yielding act that puts us within the erotic reduction. Following the lover's advance, Marion says the decision to love "will invade me with an affective tonality that is powerful, deep, and durable, and which, little by little or quite brutally, will contaminate the totality of my inner life: not only my emotional but also my intellectual life, not only my conscious but also my unconscious life" (*EP* 95). Books can offer us this overwhelming experience if we decide to let ourselves be "contaminated" by their unpredictable effect. They can make forgetting ourselves and attending to another a regular part of our daily practice and thereby strengthen in us the habit of empathy.

Works of fiction or poetry encourage us as readers to let ourselves be overtaken because they call to us with an individual voice. They portray physical, emotional, and intellectual elements as fully integrated, and through the narrator or lyric speaker they voice another way of seeing that offers more than just understanding. Understanding, as Marion points out, must be universalizable in order to facilitate rational communication.[8] But being

---

[7] Antonio Gramsci, *Selections for the Prison Notebooks*, trans. Quintin Hoare and Geoffrey Nowell-Smith (New York: International Publishers, 1971), 324.

[8] Marion, *In Excess*, 97; and *EP* 39.

universal, understanding lacks the individuality that is necessary to initiate the erotic phenomenon. By offering more than understanding, by confronting us with a whole way of seeing and experiencing the world, literature invites the lover's surrender.

Is all of this unreasonably hopeful? Yes. Love always is.

Bibliography

Abrams, M. H. *A Glossary of Literary Terms*. 7th edition. Boston: Heinle and Heinle, 1999.

Adorno, Theodor W. *Notes on Literature: Volume One*. Translated by Sherry Weber Nicholsen and edited by Rolf Tiedemann. New York: Columbia University Press, 1991.

Altieri, Charles. "The Hermeneutics of Literary Indeterminacy." *New Literary History* 10, no. 1 (1978): 71–99.

Aristotle. *Poetics*. Translated by Stephen Halliwell. Cambridge, MA: Harvard University Press, 1995.

Asad, Talal, Wendy Brown, Judith Butler, and Saba Mahmood, eds. *Is Critique Secular? Blasphemy, Injury, and Free Speech*. Berkeley: Townsend Center for the Humanities, 2009.

Attridge, Derek. *The Singularity of Literature*. London: Routledge, 2004.

Bachelard, Gaston. *The Poetics of Space*. Translated by Maria Jolas. Boston: Beacon Press, 1994.

Badiou, Alain. *Conditions*. Translated by Steve Corcoran. London: Continuum, 2008.

Badiou, Alain. *In Praise of Love*. Translated by Peter Bush. New York: New Press, 2012.

Bakhtin, Mikail. *The Dialogic Imagination: Four Essays by M. M. Bakhtin*. Translated by Caryl Emerson and Michael Holquist and edited by Michael Holquist. Austin: University of Texas Press, 1981.

Baldwin, James. "Sonny's Blues." *The Oxford Book of American Short Stories*. Edited by Joyce Carol Oates. Oxford: Oxford University Press, 1992. 408–439.

Benjamin, Walter. *Illuminations*. Translated by Harry Zohn. New York: Schoken, 1969.

Bhabha, Homi. *Location of Culture*. London: Routledge, 2012.

Blair, Sarah. "Ellison, Photography and the Origins of Invisibility." *The Cambridge Companion to Ralph Ellison*. Cambridge: Cambridge University Press, 2005. 56–81.

Boundas, Constantin V., ed. *Columbia Companion to Twentieth-Century Philosophies*. New York: Columbia University Press, 2009.

Boyd, Melba Joyce. *Wrestling with the Muse: Dudley Randall and the Broadside Press*. New York: Columbia University Press, 2003.

Brown, Wendy. "Introduction." *Is Critique Secular? Blasphemy, Injury, and Free Speech*. Edited by Talal Asad, Wendy Brown, Judith Butler, and Saba Mahmood. Berkeley: Townsend Center for the Humanities, 2009. 1–19.

Buell, Lawrence. "Introduction: In Pursuit of Ethics." *PMLA* 114, no. 1 (January 1999): 7–19.

Butler, Judith. *Senses of the Subject*. New York: Fordham University Press, 2015.

Caracciolo, Marco. "Narrative, Meaning, Interpretation: An Enactivist Approach." *Phenomenology and the Cognitive Sciences* 11, no. 3 (2012): 367–384.

Carlson, Thomas A. "Blindness and the Decision to See: On Revelation and Reception in Jean-Luc Marion." *Counter-Experiences: Reading Jean-Luc Marion*. Edited by Kevin Hart. Notre Dame, IN: University of Notre Dame Press, 2007. 153–179.

Connor, Steven. "Making an Issue of Cultural Phenomenology." *Critical Inquiry* 42, no. 1 (2000): 2–6.

Coplan, Amy. "Empathic Engagement with Narrative Fictions." *The Journal of Aesthetics and Art Criticism* 62, no. 2. (Spring 2004): 141–152.

Cummings, Edward Estlin. *E. E. Cummings Complete Poems: 1904–1962*. Edited by George J. Firmage. New York: Liveright, 1994. 97–98.

Cussett, François. "Unthinkable Readers: The Political Blindspot of French Literature." *New Literary History* 44 (2013): 260–261.

Davidson, Donald. *Inquiries into Truth and Interpretation*. Oxford: Oxford University Press, 2001.

Davis, Colin. *Critical Excess: Overreading in Derrida, Deleuze, Levinas, Žižek and Cavell*. Stanford: Stanford University Press, 2010.

de Beauvoir, Simone. *The Second Sex*. Translated by Constance Borde and Sheila Malovany-Chevallier. New York: Vintage, 2011.

Derrida, Jacques. "Différance." Translated by Alan Bass, *Margins of Philosophy*. Chicago: University of Chicago Press, 1982. 3–27.

Derrida, Jacques. *On Touching: Jean-Luc Nancy*. Translated by Christine Irizarry. Stanford: Standford University Press, 2005.

Derrida, Jacques. "Restitutions of the Truth in Pointing." *The Art of Art History: A Critical Anthology*. Edited by Donald Preziosi. Oxford: Oxford University Press, 2009. 301–315.

Derrida, Jacques. *The Politics of Friendship*. London: Verso, 2005.

Derrida, Jacques and Jean-Luc Marion. "On the Gift: A Discussion between Jacques Derrida and Jean-Luc Marion Moderated by Richard Kearney." *God, the Gift, and*

Postmodernism. Edited by John Caputo and Michael J. Scanlon. Bloomington, IN: Indiana University Press, 1999. 54–78.

de Vries, Hent. *Minimal Theologies: Critiques of Secular Reason*. 2nd edition. Translated by Geoffrey Hale. Baltimore: Johns Hopkins University Press, 2005.

Eaglestone, Robert. *Ethical Criticism: Reading after Levinas*. Edinburgh: Edinburgh University Press, 1997.

Eagleton, Terry. "It Is Not Quite True That I Have a Body, and Not Quite True That I Am One Either." Review of Peter Brooks's *Body Work*. *London Review of Books* 15, no. 10 (1993).

Eagleton, Terry. *The Event of Literature*. New Haven, CT: Yale University Press, 2013.

Eldridge, Richard. "Introduction." *The Oxford Handbook of Philosophy and Literature*. Edited by Richard Eldridge. Oxford: Oxford University Press, 2009. 1–9.

Ellison, Ralph. *Invisible Man*. New York: Vintage, 1995.

Falke, Cassandra. "Good Reading: An Ethics of Christian Literary Theory." *Intersections*. Edited by Cassandra Falke. Basingstoke: Palgrave Macmillan, 2010. 46–56.

Falke, Cassandra, ed. *Intersections in Christianity and Critical Theory*. Basingstoke: Palgrave Macmillan, 2010.

Falke, Cassandra. *Literature by the Working Class: English Autobiography, 1820–1848*. Amherst: Cambria, 2013.

Farner, Geir. *Literary Fiction: The Ways We Read Narrative Literature*. New York: Bloomsbury, 2014.

Faulkner, William. *Absalom! Absalom!* New York: Modern Library, 2012.

Felski, Rita. "Critique and the Hermeneutic of Suspicion." *M/C Journal: A Journal of Media and Culture* 15, no. 1 (2012).

Felski, Rita. *The Uses of Literature*. Oxford: Blackwell, 2008.

Ferretter, Luke. *Towards a Christian Literary Theory*. Basingstoke: Palgrave Macmillan, 2003.

Fish, Stanley. "Interpreting the Variorum." *Critical Inquiry* 2 (1976): 465–485.

Gadamer, Hans-George. *Truth and Method*. Translated by Joel Weinsheimer and Donald G. Marshall. London: Bloomsbury, 2013.

Gioia, Dana. "Preface." *Reading at Risk: A Survey of Literary Reading in America—Executive Summary*. Washington, DC: National Endowment for the Arts, 2002.

Glendenning, Simon and Robert Eaglestone, eds. *Derrida's Legacies: Literature and Philosophy*. London: Routledge, 2008.

Godwin, William. *Things as They Are, or The Adventures of Caleb Williams*. Edited by Maurice Hindle. London: Penguin, 1988.

Goh, Irving. *The Reject: Community, Politics and Religion after the Subject.*
New York: Fordham University Press, 2015.

Gramsci, Antonio. *Selections for the Prison Notebooks.* Translated by Quintin Hoare
and Geoffrey Nowell-Smith. New York: International Publishers, 1971.

Gschwandtner, Christina. *Degrees of Givenness: On Saturation in Jean-Luc Marion.*
Bloomington, IN: Indiana University Press, 2014.

Gustavson, Malena. "Bisexuals in Relationships: Uncoupling Intimacy from
*Gender Ontology." Bisexual and Queer Theory: Intersections, Connections and
Challenges.* Edited by Jonathan Alexander and Serena Anderlini-D'Onofrio.
London: Routledge, 2014. 215–237.

Habermas, Jürgen. "Secularism's Crisis of Faith: Notes on Post-Secular Society." *New
Perspectives Quarterly* 25 (2008): 17–29.

Hamid, Mohsin. "Living in the Age of Permawar." *The Guardian,* August 22, 2015.

Hammond, Meghan Marie and Sue J. Kim, eds. *Rethinking Empathy through
Literature.* New York: Routledge, 2014.

Hans, James S. "Gaston Bachelard and the Phenomenology of the Reading
Consciousness." *The Journal of Aesthetics and Art Criticism* 35, no. 3 (Spring,
1977): 315–327.

Hart, Kevin. "Afterword." *Christianity and Literature* 58, no. 2 (2009): 295–303.

Hart, Kevin. *Counter-Experiences: Reading Jean-Luc Marion.* Notre Dame,
IN: University of Notre Dame Press, 2007.

Hart, Kevin. "Introduction." *Jean-Luc Marion: Essential Writings.* New York:
Fordham University Press, 2013. 1–38.

Hart, Kevin. "It/Is True." *Studia Phenomenologica* 8 (2008): 219–239.

Hazlitt, William. *Characters of Shakespeare's Plays.* London: John Templeton, 1838.

Hazlitt, William. *The Spirit of the Age, or Contemporary Portraits.* London: Colburn,
1825.

Heidegger, Martin. *Being and Time.* Translated by John Macquarrie and Edward
Robinson. Oxford: Blackwell, 1962.

Heidegger, Martin. "The Origin of the Work of Art." *Basic Writings.* Translated by Albert
Hofstadter and edited by David Farrell Krell. London: Routledge, 1993. 143–212.

Heidegger, Martin. "What is Called Thinking?" Translated by J. Glenn Gray. New
York: Perennial, 1976.

Hogan, Patrick Colm. "The Epilogue of Suffering: Heroism, Empathy, Ethics"
SubStance. 30, nos. 1–2 (2001): 119–143.

Hogan, Patrick Colm. *Affective Narratology: The Emotional Structure of Stories.*
Lincoln: University of Nebraska Press, 2011.

Hooton, Jessica. "After Theory, After Modernity: Reading Humbly." *Intersections in Christianity and Critical Theory*. Edited by Cassandra Falke. 23–32.

Horner, Robyn. *Jean-Luc Marion: A Theological Introduction*. Aldershot: Ashgate Press, 2005.

Hsu, Chun-Ting, Markusa Conrad, and Arthur Jacobs. "Fiction Feelings in Harry Potter: Haemodynamic Response in the Mid-Cingulate Cortex Correlates With Immersive Reading Experience." *NeuroReport* 25, no. 17 (December 2014): 1356–1361.

Husserl, Edmund. *Ideas: General Introduction to Pure Phenomenology*. Translated by Dermot Moran. London: Routledge, 2012.

Husserl, Edmund. "Letter to Hoftmannsthal." Translated by Sven-Olov Wallenstein. *Site* 27–29 (2009): 2.

Husserl, Edmund. *Logical Investigations*. 2 vols. Translated by Dermot Moran. New York: Routledge, 2001.

Husserl, Edmund. *On Phantasy, Image, Consciousness and Memory*. Translated by John B. Brough. *Collected Works*, Vol. II. Dordrecht: Springer, 2005.

Husserl, Edmund. *Paris Lectures*. Translated by Peter Koestenbaum. Dordrecht: Springer, 1964.

Husserl, Edmund. *The Crisis of the European Sciences and Transcendental Phenomenology*. Translated by David Carr. Evanston: Northwestern University Press, 1970.

Husserl, Edmund. *The Essential Husserl: Basic Writings in Transcendental Phenomenology*. Edited by Donn Welton. Bloomington, IN: Indiana University Press, 1999.

Iser, Wolfgang. *The Act of Reading: A Theory of Aesthetic Response*. Baltimore: Johns Hopkins, 1978.

Iser, Wolfgang. "The Reading Process: A Phenomenological Approach." *New Literary History* 3, no. 2 (Winter 1972): 279–299.

Jacobs, Alan. *A Theology of Reading: The Hermeneutics of Love*. Boulder, CO: Westview Press, 2001.

James, Ian. *The New French Philosophy*. London: Polity Press, 2012.

Jameson, Frederic. *The Cultural Turn: Selected Writings on the Postmodern, 1983–1998*. London: Verso, 1998.

Janicaud, Dominique, Jean-Francois Courtine, Jean-Louis Chrétien, Michel Henry, Jean-Luc Marion, and Paul Ricoeur. *Phenomenology and the Theological Turn: The French Debate*. New York: Fordham University Press, 2000.

Johnson, Dan. "Transportation into a Story Increases Empathy, Prosocial Behavior, and Perceptual Bias toward Fearful Expressions." *Personality and Individual Differences* 52, no. 2 (2012): 150–155.

Jurecic, Ann. "Empathy and the Critic." *College English* 74, no. 1 (2011): 10–27.

Kandinsky, Wassily. *On the Spiritual in Art*. Edited and translated by Hilla Rebay. New York: Guggenheim Foundation, 1946.

Kant, Immanuel. *Critique of the Power of Judgment*. Translated by James Meredith and edited by Nicolas Walker. Oxford: Oxford University Press, 2007.

Keen, Suzanne. *Empathy and the Novel*. Oxford: Oxford University Press, 2007.

Kosofsky-Sedgwick, Eve. *Touching Feeling: Affect, Pedagogy, Performativity*. Durham: Duke University Press, 2003.

Landy, Joshua. *How To Do Things with Fictions*. Oxford: Oxford University Press, 2012.

Landy, Joshua and Michael Saler, eds. *Re-enchantment of the World: Secular Magic in a Rational Age*. Stanford: Stanford University Press, 2009.

Lévinas, Emmanuel. *Ethics and Infinity: Conversations with Philippe Nemo*. Translated by Richard Cohen. Pittsburgh: Duquesne University Press, 1985.

Lévinas, Emmanuel. "Signature." Edited by Adrian Peperzak. *Research in Phenomenology* 8 (January 1978): 175–189.

Lévinas, Emmanuel. *Totality and Infinity: Essays on Exteriority*. Translated by Alphonso Lingis. Dordrecht: Kluwer Academic Press, 1991.

Lewis, Michael and Tanja Staehler. *Phenomenology: An Introduction*. London: Continuum, 2010.

Lorang, Elizabeth. "Not Feeling Very Well … We Turned our Attention to Poetry: Poetry, Hospital Newspapers, and the Civil War." *Literature and Journalism: Inspiration, Intersections, and Inventions from Ben Franklin to Stephen Colbert*. Edited by Mark Canada. Basingstoke: Palgrave Macmillan, 2013. 69–89.

Lukács, György. *Soul and Form*. Edited by John T. Sanders and Katie Terezakis. New York: Columbia University Press, 2010.

Manguel, Alberto. *A Reader in the Looking-Glass Wood: Essays on Books, Reading and the World*. San Diego: Harcourt, 1998.

Manguel, Alberto. *A Reader on Reading*. New Haven: Yale University Press, 2010.

Mar, Raymond and Keith Oatley. "The Function of Fiction is the Abstraction and Simulation of Social Experience." *Perspectives on Psychological Science* 3, no. 3 (2008): 173–192.

Mar, Raymond A., Keith Oatley, Jacob Hirsh, Jennifer dela Paz, and Jordan B. Peterson. "Bookworms Versus Nerds: Exposure to Fiction Versus Non-Fiction,

Divergent Associations with Social Ability, and the Simulation of Fictional Social Worlds." *Journal of Research in Personality* 40, no. 5 (October 2006): 694–712.

Marion, Jean-Luc. "The Banality of Saturation." *Counter-Experiences*. Edited by Kevin Hart. Notre Dame, IN: University of Notre Dame Press, 2007. 383–418.

Marion, Jean-Luc. *Being Given: Toward a Phenomenology of Givenness*. Translated by Jeffrey L. Kosky. Stanford: Stanford University Press, 2002.

Marion, Jean-Luc. *The Crossing of the Visible*. Translated by James K. A. Smith. Stanford: Stanford University Press, 2004.

Marion, Jean-Luc. *The Erotic Phenomenon*. Translated by Stephen E. Lewis. Chicago: University of Chicago Press, 2007.

Marion, Jean-Luc. "The Event, the Phenomenon and the Revealed." *Transcendence in Philosophy and Religion*. Edited by James E. Faulconer. Bloomington, IN: Indiana University Press, 2003. 87–105.

Marion, Jean-Luc. *Givenness and Hermeneutics*. Translated by Jean-Pierre Lafouge. Milwaukee, WI: Marquette University Press, 2013.

Marion, Jean-Luc. *God without Being*. Translated by Thomas A. Carlson. Chicago: University of Chicago Press, 1991.

Marion, Jean-Luc. *The Idol and the Distance: Five Studies*. Translated by Thomas A. Carlson and edited by John D. Caputo. New York: Fordham University Press, 2001.

Marion, Jean-Luc. *In the Self's Place: The Approach of St. Augustine*. Translated by Jeffrey Kosky. Stanford: Stanford University Press, 2012.

Marion, Jean-Luc. *In Excess: Studies of Saturated Phenomena*. Translated by Robyn Horner and Vincent Berraud. New York: Fordham University Press, 2002.

Marion, Jean-Luc. *Prolegomena to Charity*. Translated by Stephen E. Lewis. New York: Fordham University Press, 2002.

Marion, Jean-Luc. *Reduction and Givenness: Investigations of Husserl, Heidegger and Phenomenology*. Translated by Thomas A. Carlson. Evanston, IL: Northwestern University Press, 1998.

Marion, Jean-Luc. "Resting, Moving, Loving: The Access to the Self According to Saint Augustine." *The Journal of Religion* 91, no. 9 (January 2011): 24–42.

Marion, Jean-Luc. "The Saturated Phenomenon." *Philosophy Today* 40, no. 1 (1996): 103–124.

Marion, Jean-Luc. *The Visible and the Revealed*. Translated by Christina M. Gschwandtner. New York: Fordham University Press, 2008.

Marion, Jean-Luc and Richard Kearney. "A Dialogue with Jean-Luc Marion." *Philosophy Today* 48, no. 1 (Spring 2004): 12–26.

Marx, Karl. "Contribution to the Critique of Hegel's Philosophy of Right, Introduction." *The Marx-Engels Reader.* Edited by Robert Tucker. New York: Norton, 1978.

McLennen, Gregor. "The Postsecular Turn." *Theory, Culture & Society* 27, no. 4 (July 2010): 3–20.

Merleau-Ponty, Maurice. *Phenomenology of Perception.* Translated by Colin Smith. London: Routledge, 2002.

Merleau-Ponty, Maurice. *The Visible and the Invisible.* Translated by Alphonso Lingis. Evanston, IL: Northwestern University Press, 1969.

Michaels, Anne. *Fugitive Pieces.* London: Bloomsbury, 1997.

Mikkola, Mari. "Ontological Commitments, Sex and Gender." *Feminist Metaphysics: Explorations in the Ontology of Sex, Gender and the Self.* Edited by Charlotte Witt. New York: Springer, 2011. 67–83.

Milbank, John. "The Gift and the Mirror." *Counter-Experiences: Reading Jean-Luc Marion.* Edited by Kevin Hart. Notre Dame, IN: University of Notre Dame Press, 2007. 253–317.

Milosz, Czeslaw. *The Witness of Poetry.* Cambridge, MA: Harvard University Press, 1983.

Moran, Dermot. "Editor's Introduction." *The Phenomenology Reader.* Edited by Dermot Moran. London: Routledge, 2002. 1–26.

Moran, Dermot. *Introduction to Phenomenology.* London: Routledge, 2000.

Morrison, Toni. *The Bluest Eye.* London: Vintage, 1999.

Nussbaum, Martha. *Cultivating Humanity: A Classical Defense of Reform in Liberal Education.* Cambridge, MA: Harvard University Press, 1997.

Nussbaum, Martha. *Love's Knowledge: Essays on Philosophy and Literature.* Oxford: Oxford University Press, 1990.

Pascal, Janet. *Arthur Conan Doyle: Beyond Baker Street.* Oxford: Oxford University Press, 2000.

Pater, Walter. *Studies in the History of the Renaissance.* Oxford: Oxford University Press, 2010.

Phillips, Natalie. "Literary Neuroscience and the History of Attention: An fMRI Study of Reading Jane Austen." *The Oxford Handbook for Cognitive Approaches to Literature.* Edited by Lisa Zunshine. Oxford: Oxford University Press, 2015.

Poulet, Georges. "The Phenomenology of Reading." *New Literary History* 1, no. 1 (October 1969): 53–68.

Rancière, Jacques. "A Few Remarks on the Method of Jacques Rancière." *Parallax* 15, no. 3 (2009): 114–123.

Rancière, Jacques. *The Flesh of Words: The Politics of Writing*. Translated by Charlotte Mandell. Stanford: Stanford University Press, 2004.

Randall, Dudley. "The Ballad of Birmingham." *Cities Burning*. Detroit, MI: Broadside Press, 1968.

Ray, Rebecca, Milla Sanes, and John Schmitt. "No Vacation Nation Revisited." Center for Economic and Policy Research (May 2013). 1–24.

Ricoeur, Paul. *Critique and Conviction*. Translated by Kathleen Blamey. New York: Columbia University Press, 1998.

Ricoeur, Paul. *From Text to Action: Essays in Hermeneutics II*. Translated by Kathleen Blamey and John B. Thompson. Evanston, IL: Northwestern University Press, 1991.

Ricoeur, Paul. *Oneself as Another*. Translated by Kathleen Blamey. Chicago: University of Chicago Press, 1992.

Robbins, Jill. *Altered Reading: Levinas and Literature*. Chicago: University of Chicago, 1999.

Robinette, Brian. "A Gift to Theology? Jean-Luc Marion's 'Saturated Phenomenon' in Christological Perspective." *Heythrop Journal* 48, no. 1 (2007): 86–108.

Scheler, Max. *Formalism in Ethics and Non-Formal Ethics of Values: A New Attempt toward the Foundation of an Ethical Personalism*. Translated by Manfred Frings and Robert L. Funk. Evanston, IL: Northwestern University Press, 1973.

Schwartz, Regina, ed. *Transcendence: Philosophy, Literature, and Theology Approach the Beyond*. London: Routledge, 2007.

Sokolowski, Robert. *Introduction to Phenomenology*. Cambridge: Cambridge University Press, 1999.

Spiegelberg, Herbert and Erwin Speigelberg. *The Phenomenological Movement: A Historical Introduction*. Dordrecht: Kluwer, 1981.

Steiner, George. *Real Presences: Is There Anything in What We Say?* Chicago: University of Chicago, 1989.

Stevenson, Robert Louis. *Treasure Island*. Oxford: Oxford University Press, 2011.

Stewart, Susan. "Romantic Meter and Form." *Cambridge Companion to British Romantic Poetry*. Cambridge: Cambridge University Publishing, 2008. 53–75.

Suhor, Charles. "Contemplative Reading—The Experience, the Idea, the Applications." *The English Journal* 91, no. 4 (March 2002): 28–32.

Taylor, Charles. *A Secular Age*. Cambridge, MA: Harvard University Press, 2007.

Thompson, Helen and Shakar Vedantam. "A Lively Mind: Your Brain on Jane Austen." *Morning Edition. NPR* (16 October 2012).

Thomson, Christopher. *The Autobiography of an Artisan.* London: Chapman, 1847.

Tóth, Beáta. "Love Between Embodiment and Spirituality: Jean-Luc Marion and John Paul II on Erotic Love." *Modern Theology* 29 (2013): 18–47.

Vlacos, Sophie. *Ricoeur, Literature and Imagination.* New York: Bloomsbury Press, 2014.

Waugh, Evelyn. *Brideshead Revisited: The Sacred and Profane Memories of Captain Charles Ryder.* London: Chapman and Hall, 1972.

Wehrs, Donald R. *Levinas and Twentieth-Century Literature: Ethics and the Reconstitution of Subjectivity.* Newark: University of Delaware Press, 2013.

Wiesel, Elie. *Night.* New York: Bantam Books, 2000.

Wiskus, Jessica. *The River of Thought: Literature and Music after Merleau-Ponty.* Chicago: University of Chicago Press, 2015.

Woolf, Virginia. "Modern Novels." *The Essays of Virginia Woolf.* Edited by Andrew McNeillie. 6 vols. London: Hogarth Press, 1986: iii, 30–37.

Wordsworth, William. "Lines Written a Few Miles Above Tintern Abbey." *The Major Works.* Edited by Stephen Gill. Oxford: Oxford University Press, 2008. 131–135.

Zahavi, Dan. "Beyond Empathy: Phenomenological Approaches to Intersubjectivity." *Journal of Consciousness Studies* 8, nos. 5–7 (2001): 151–167.

Zahavi, Dan. *Husserl's Phenomenology.* Stanford: Stanford University Press, 2003.

Zunshine, Lisa. *Why We Read Fiction: Theory of Mind and the Novel.* Columbus: Ohio State University Press, 2006.

Index